PELICAN BOOKS

UNEMPLOYMENT

Kevin Hawkins was educated at Keighley Grammar School and Gonville and Caius College, Cambridge, where he obtained a double first-class honours degree. He spent a year doing research at Nuffield College, Oxford, and then joined the research staff of the University of Bradford Management Centre and was appointed Lecturer in Industrial Relations in 1970. He is an associate member of the British Institute of Management, has acted as consultant to several organizations and has worked extensively in the field of management training and development. Kevin Hawkins's previous publications include *Conflict and Change* (1972), *Business and Society* (1974, Pelican), *British Industrial Relations 1945–75*, *The Management of Industrial Relations* (1978, Pelican) and numerous articles and contributions to other books.

KEVIN HAWKINS

UNEMPLOYMENT

PENGUIN BOOKS

Penguin Books Ltd, Harmondsworth, Middlesex, England
Penguin Books, 625 Madison Avenue, New York, New York 10022, U.S.A.
Penguin Books Australia Ltd, Ringwood, Victoria, Australia
Penguin Books Canada Ltd, 2801 John Street, Markham, Ontario, Canada L3R 1B4
Penguin Books (N.Z.) Ltd, 182–190 Wairau Road, Auckland 10, New Zealand

—

First published 1979

—

—

Made and printed in Great Britain by
Richard Clay (The Chaucer Press) Ltd,
Bungay, Suffolk
Set in Monotype Times

Contents

Preface

This book was written during the summer of 1978. Since then the level of registered unemployment in Britain has fallen slightly as a result of the moderate stimulus to economic activity administered by the Labour government in 1978. Economic forecasters are agreed, however, that the prospects for growth in the UK economy in the short-to-medium term are bleak. The fundamental nature of Britain's unemployment problem, therefore, remains as it was when this book was written.

The only significant change is the election of a Conservative government which is pledged to reverse many of its predecessor's policies. The government's main objective is to strenghthen the market sector of the economy by reducing taxation, thereby providing greater incentives to investment and growth. Obviously this will entail severe restrictions on the growth of employment in the non-market sector (mainly public services) and a much more selective use of employment subsidies. It seems certain, therefore, that over the next two or three years aggregate unemployment will rise once again, probably to new post-war heights, as the economy adjusts both to the government's strategy and to the projected recession in world trade. Whether this increase proves to be permanent will depend partly on the long-term effectiveness of the strategy (assuming it is maintained), partly on the extent to which the government can correct the most glaring mismatches in the labour market, and partly on events outside the UK. Any further crystal-gazing would at this stage be inappropriate. What does seem clear, however, is that, with the Labour Party in opposition, the level of unemployment will become a much more emotive political issue than it has been in the recent past.

In conclusion, I would like to thank Professor Thomas Kempner for reading the manuscript of this book in draft form and Mrs Jo Baxter for typing it.

Kevin Hawkins

University of Bradford Management Centre,
May 1979

CHAPTER ONE

Introduction

Unemployment arises because, while the supply of labour grows steadily, the demand for labour, in growing, varies incessantly in volume, distribution and character. This variation, in several of its forms at least, flows directly from the control of production by many competing employers. It is obvious that so long as the world is split up into separate groups of producers – each group with a life of its own, and growing or decaying in ceaseless attrition on its neighbours – there must be insecurity of employment. It is probable that at least one of the most striking specific factors in the problem – namely, cyclical fluctuation of trade – may be traced ultimately to this same source. Unemployment, in other words, is to some extent at least part of the price of industrial competition – part of the waste without which there would be no competition at all.

W. H. Beveridge, 1909

All industrial societies must live with a certain degree of unemployment. The problem for policy-makers is to define what they consider to be an acceptable level of unemployment and justify this definition to the electorate. In the post-war period unemployment throughout the Western world was, by historical standards, extremely low. Politicians and voters alike soon grew accustomed to the belief that at least 98 per cent of those who were willing and able to work should at all times have a job. If unemployment rose above this level, it was generally believed that the government of the day had a moral as well as a political duty to increase the level of economic activity. Since the late 1960s, however, the 'normal' level of unemployment both in the UK and Western Europe as a whole has risen, and the ability of governments to reverse this trend by expansionist fiscal and monetary policies is now in doubt. No politician has yet dared say that 'full' employment might in future mean that only 94 per cent of those who are willing and able to work can reasonably expect to have a job. But economists have been less reticent. The Cambridge Economic Policy Group, for example, has predicted that unless current economic policies are changed there will be over 3 million unemployed by 1985. Other researchers have forecast that by the end of the century unemployment may well be around the 5 million mark. In a society which for more than twenty years after the Second World War prided itself on being fully employed, such predictions must surely give cause for concern.

The general reaction to higher unemployment has, however, been remarkably muted in tone. Does this suggest that an average unemployment rate of, say, 6 per cent is not as intolerable as we once assumed it would be? After all, in 1976–8 Britain's unemployment rate hovered around this level and the minority Labour government of the day remained in office without too much difficulty. For the vast majority of workers who kept their jobs, as for the government itself, the main economic problem was – and still is – inflation rather than unemployment. This may be attributed in part to the belief – now firmly held in Whitehall and Westminster – that if inflation begins to accelerate once again it will lead to even higher unemployment. It also reflects the fear, equally widespread in official circles, that any attempt to reduce unemployment by means of a major reflationary package will, as in 1972–3, simply suck in more imports and undermine foreign confidence in sterling. The attitude of the public as a whole seems ambiguous. On the one hand, opinion polls suggest that many people instinctively dislike the idea of deliberately creating unemployment in order to restrain inflation. On the other hand, many people also seem to believe that the 'generous' welfare payments now available to those out of work have effectively broken the old link between unemployment and poverty and have thereby removed the financial incentive for the unemployed to seek work. In short, it is widely believed that the dole queues of today are not really comparable with those of the 1930s and should not therefore arouse too much sympathy.

The disappearance of full employment as we knew it up to the mid-1960s has thus been accepted with remarkable equanimity.

Indeed, it has become fashionable to argue that Western society will have to live with a permanently higher level of unemployment for the rest of the century. Those who propound this argument can marshal some persuasive evidence. They can point, for example, to the underlying tendency for many industries and services to become more capital-intensive. Since the late 1960s the relationship between unemployment and output has undoubtedly changed so that a steadily smaller stock of manpower is now required to produce a given volume of goods and services. To the extent that this trend is the product of technological change, it implies that the demand for labour will become increasingly specialist in character so that men and women who do not possess the appropriate skills and have little aptitude to acquire them will find it increasingly difficult to obtain work. A more optimistic view of technological change might, however, suggest that while fewer and fewer people will be in full-time employment, they will be able to produce a far greater volume of goods and services than is currently possible. Not only will those in work have more leisure time at their disposal, but a richer society will be able to support a higher level of unemployment without undue discomfort.

If we could be sure that technological change will indeed confer such benefits on society, there would be some justification for regarding our current unemployment problem as simply a transitional cost. Unfortunately the optimists' vision of a richer, more leisured society begs a few awkward questions. Firstly, technological change will only make Britain richer if we are in the vanguard of such change and are successful in selling new products in the international market place. Unless these conditions are fulfilled Britain will be a net loser, as indeed it has been up to the present time. Secondly, the optimists seem to be assuming that most people actually want more leisure and, in the case of the unemployed, that they will accept almost permanent leisure. The problem is that someone can only enjoy increased leisure time if he has enough income to spend on the leisure pursuits of his choice. Enforced leisure on an inadequate income would hardly be an attractive proposition. This argument also raises the difficult question of how the social and psychological role of work is to be displaced. There is no space here for a disquisition on the 'puritan ethic', but it is at least arguable that for most people the possession of a job is a salient part of their lives. The assumption which guides the labour market policies of all Western governments is that most of those who are out of work would prefer to have a job and do not like to regard themselves – or be regarded by society – as 'welfare parasites'. It is of course conceivable that this assumption is mistaken, but as yet there is very little evidence to suggest that it is. It would therefore be more honest to recognize that at present no one knows what the long-term effects of technological change on the pattern and level of employment will be.

Policy-makers and the various groups who seek to influence them are essentially preoccupied with Britain's current unemployment problem and the prospects of alleviating it in the short-to-medium term. On the left of the political spectrum there is general support for extended state intervention in order to prevent any further increase in unemployment. Thus since 1974 the Labour government has taken steps to preserve jobs which would otherwise have disappeared and has in addition created thousands of jobs which would not otherwise have existed. This strategy has attracted much criticism from right-wing politicians and economists, who tend to argue that employment subsidies are at best cosmetic and at worst damaging to productivity and industrial mobility. There is a large measure of bipartisan support for the belated attempts which have been made to increase the flow of skilled manpower. But it is also generally agreed that while enhanced training facilities will help to correct the 'mismatches' which currently exist between supply and demand in the labour market, they will not in themselves have more than a marginal effect on the future growth of employment. This, of course, is the fundamental question facing all politicians and economists – how can we achieve an employment growth rate which will be sufficient to absorb the projected increase in the supply of labour and at the same time keep inflation under control, protect the balance of payments and improve industrial efficiency?

One school of thought, broadly associated with the right-wing Institute for Economic Affairs and ably represented in Parliament by Sir Keith Joseph, has in effect answered this question by denying that a real problem exists. This school argues that the aggregate unemployment statistics give a misleading impression of the real state of the labour market. Some of their criticisms of these statistics are certainly valid. They are right, for example, to remind us that the monthly count of the registered unemployed is only a snapshot of a dynamic situation and that the number of people on the register at any given time does not represent a large, stagnant pool of unemployment. They are also broadly correct in emphasizing the need to differentiate between the labour market situation of specific groups such as women, school-leavers, the old, the skilled and so on. Their attempts to construct a new and allegedly more realistic index of 'real' unemployment are, however, much more questionable. Indeed, it will be argued in the course of this book that Britain's current unemployment problem cannot be solved simply by re-arranging the relevant statistics.

With all their weaknesses, the official figures still provide us with valuable information about the changing balance between supply and demand in the labour market and thus throw *some* light on the nature of Britain's unemployment problem. Firstly, they suggest that long-term unemployment is increasing, particularly among men. Secondly, they suggest that the rate of unemployment among young people has been rising, so that the young are now disproportionately represented among the un-employed. Thirdly, they indicate that the occupational distribu-tion of unemployment is, as always, highly uneven. Finally they suggest that while regional differences in unemployment rates are not as significant as they used to be, an acute structural imbalance is emerging in many inner urban labour markets. In general, it would seem that mismatches between those jobs that are available and the characteristics of the unemployed have become increasingly pronounced in recent years. What the official statistics do *not* disclose, however, is that level of un-employment at which the economy may be regarded as fully employed. While it is generally believed that the demand for labour has changed both qualitatively and quantitatively in recent years, it must also be admitted that at present we know far too little about why these changes have occurred and thus about the likely shape of future trends.

A Marxist, of course would be unlikely to attach much importance to deficiencies in the official statistics. He would argue that successive governments have deliberately created unemployment in order to curb the bargaining power of organized labour and protect the profits of capitalists. Draconian incomes policies, restrictive labour legislation and higher unemployment must all be seen as part of a general strategy designed to hold down the working class. The growth of structural unemployment may also be fitted into a Marxist analysis in so far as it suggests that the capitalist system, driven on by the pressure of technological change and the need for higher profits, will require less and less labour power. The inevitable result of these internal contradictions will be a gradual breakdown of the existing order. Those readers who are not blessed with the same degree of certainty about the future, however, may wish to approach the problem from a different standpoint.

The first step is to examine the performance of the British economy over the past thirty years and project its underlying growth rate against the anticipated trend in the supply of labour. The inference is that the future trend in unemployment will be inexorably upward, at least until the end of the century. If this is to be avoided, the underlying growth rate of the economy must be radically improved. The key to this desirable objective lies in raising the low average level of productivity in British industry to something like that of our major industrial competitors. But in view of the projected trend towards more capital-intensive methods of production and the scope which currently exists for increasing output with the *same* labour force, there is likely to be a further net loss of jobs in the private sector of the economy in the short-to-medium term. In theory the growing manpower surplus could be absorbed by an expansion of labour-intensive forms of employment in the public sector. Such an expansion is, however, extremely unlikely in view of the implications it would have for the general level of public expenditure and thus for the rate of inflation. Only in the private service sector can we reasonably predict further expansion and even here the demand for labour may become increasingly specific to certain groups. In general, therefore, it is difficult to see how the economy will, on its track record to date, generate enough jobs to absorb the projected increase in the labour supply, let alone provide work for a large proportion of those who are currently unemployed.

The implications of this scenario for the quality of life in our society over the next two decades can hardly be ignored. The tendency for the 'work ethic' to lose its normative influence over individuals as the duration of their unemployment increases must be of particular concern to policy-makers. It cannot be denied that for a minority of people the present level of welfare payments has largely removed the financial sting of unemployment, but there is no evidence to suggest that the majority of the unemployed are quite content to be 'welfare parasites'. While right-wing critics are right to remind us that *some* of the long-term unemployed are virtually unemployable and that *some* of the short-term unemployed may simply be 'shopping around' for jobs, the upward trend in the average duration of unemployment must give us cause for concern. Such concern is especially warranted in the inner areas of large industrial cities and conurbations, particularly those in which there are large concentrations of young, non-white workers. Those readers who are familiar with the problems of inner-city life will not find it difficult to predict the social and political consequences of continued high unemployment in these areas. There is little point in telling those who live in a decaying urban environment and find themselves out of work for months on end that they should be enjoying the leisure time which technological progress has conferred upon them. Increased leisure will not appeal either to the unemployed or to those who have jobs unless and until it is accompanied by an appropriate level of real income.

What, then, can the government do? In theory it should be devising a macro-economic strategy whose objective is to restore full employment. The practical problems which confront policy makers are, however, immense. We shall argue that it is no longer realistic to define full employment in terms of the extremely low levels of unemployment which we experienced up to the late 1960s, yet it is very difficult to say what full employment now means in precise, quantitative terms. Consequently politicians and economists alike are now trying to chart a course through unfamiliar waters, and in these circumstances it is easy to find fault with what has been done in recent years. Any government in practice faces a difficult choice between two quite different strategies. On the one hand, it can seek to preserve existing jobs and create enough new ones to make a real impact on the unemployment figures. This would presumably involve large subsidies to firms in difficulties, a major increase in public service employment and the widespread sharing of work. It might also entail the imposition of drastic controls on imports, as the Cambridge Economic Policy Group, the TUC and the left wing of the Labour party have been advocating for some time. In the short term such a strategy would undoubtedly reduce unemployment but the long-term cost in terms of productivity growth, output, profitability, taxation, investment, inflation and the balance of payments would be high. On the other hand, the government can seek to create a climate in which the market sector of the economy should eventually be able to generate new employment and higher real incomes. This would require a substantial cut in the tax burden, severe restraints on public expenditure, the introduction of incentives to improve productivity and the adoption of a much more selective approach to job preservation. But it would also entail a sharp increase in unemployment in the short-to-medium term which might well be politically unacceptable to any government and would certainly impose a heavy additional burden on welfare expenditure. In practice, therefore, government policy in Britain, as in other Western European countries, has sought to steer a middle course between these two contrasting strategies. The obvious danger is that public policy will never be more than a series of *ad hoc* and potentially contradictory responses. If this happens there can be little doubt that unemployment will gradually drift upwards and that by the end of the century the problem will be truly insoluble.

In the course of this short, introductory book we shall try to analyse the nature of Britain's unemployment problem and offer a tentative evaluation of the various 'solutions' which have been advanced from different points on the political spectrum. In

Chapter Two we shall introduce some of the technical terms which are used in most discussions of unemployment and examine both the nature of the aggregate unemployment statistics and the criticisms which they have recently attracted. In Chapter Three the characteristics of the unemployed and the changing composition of the labour force are analysed. These two chapters lead us to the conclusion that while Britain undoubtedly has an unemployment problem at the present time, it will not be removed by a conventional expansion of aggregate demand, even if this option were still open to policy-makers. This leads us directly into a discussion (Chapter Four) of why the economy has gradually moved away from full employment as we knew it up to the mid-1960s. A view of the likely trend in unemployment over the next decade is also presented. The final chapter is devoted to a discussion of the alternative macro-economic strategies which have been advanced with a view to containing or reducing unemployment and to an evaluation of labour market policy in Britain since 1974. The present writer has no rabbit to pull out of the hat and does not claim to have *the* solution. But by this stage of the discussion the reader will hopefully be aware that, despite some ambitious claims to the contrary, no one else has *the* solution either.

CHAPTER TWO

Does Britain Have an Unemployment Problem?

... the most important explanation for the failure of 'demand management' during the last thirty years is that the British authorities, especially the Treasury, have never fully appreciated how misleading the unemployment figures are as a test of the pressure of demand on the economy. Even if they had, the presentation of such figures has been such a gift to political demagogues that it would scarcely have been easy to introduce the appropriate policies.

John Wood, 1975

Should we worry about the level of unemployment in Britain today? The question may at first glance seem at best academic and at worst socially irresponsible. After all, the official statistics point to a steadily worsening trend in unemployment over the past decade or so. Between 1948 and 1966 the average number of people on the unemployment register was just over 350,000, or rather less than 2 per cent of all employees. Indeed, up to 1958 there was at most times *excess* demand for labour and as late as the mid-1960s the shortage of labour was generally held to be a major constraint on the rate of economic growth. The sharp deflation of the economy by the famous 'July measures' of 1966 ushered in a new era of relatively high and, it would seem, rising unemployment. Between 1967 and 1974 registered unemployment never fell below half a million and during the severe recession of 1975–8 it rose to a peak of 1·37 million (excluding school-leavers) or roughly 6 per cent of all employees.

The severity of the recent recession can, of course, be blamed on the Organization of Petroleum Exporting Countries (OPEC), which, by raising the price of oil so sharply in 1973–4, plunged the world into a severe and prolonged recession. The inference is that if the oil crisis had not occurred, unemployment would now be much lower than it is. But while it would obviously be absurd to argue that the oil price explosion has not had a major impact on employment throughout the Western world, it must also be recognized that in Britain at least the origins of our present problem can be traced back several years *before* the oil crisis. The central fact is that since the mid-1960s a given level of output of goods and services has needed a smaller stock of manpower in employment. In 1962, for example, an annual rise in output of 1·1 per cent was achieved with an official unemployment rate of 1·8 per cent. In 1976, by contrast, a similar increase in output occurred with unemployment at 5·4 per cent. The changing relationship between the level of unemployment and movements in total output is illustrated in Figure 1. Up to 1966 the year-to-year changes in this relationship looped around an unemployment rate of 1·5 per cent. Between 1966 and 1974, however, the

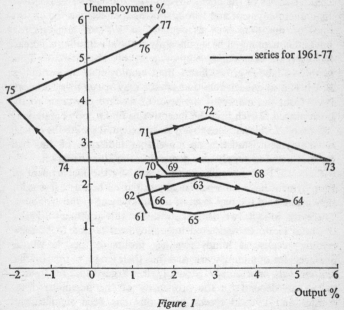

Figure 1

Unemployment rate and annual change in output, 1961–77.

Source: *CSO Economic Trends* and *Department of Employment Gazette.*

loop formed around an unemployment rate of 2·7 per cent and since 1974 the loop seems to have moved above 4 per cent. Evidence from other Western countries suggests that this upward shift in the unemployment-output relationship is by no means peculiar to Britain. To the extent that it reflects a decline in the demand for labour, the underlying causes may be technological change in particular and productivity growth in general.

The relationship between unemployment and output is not, however, the only index of changing conditions within labour markets. Since the late 1960s there has been a significant change in the relationship between unemployment and vacancies such that a given level of vacancies is now associated with a much higher level of unemployment. This may be indicative of a growing mismatch between the jobs that are available and the characteristics of the unemployed. The co-existence of relatively high unemployment and labour shortages underlines the importance of supply as well as demand factors and suggests that unemployment might be significantly reduced without an increase in aggregate demand. Unemployment may also increase if the supply of labour grows faster than employment opportunities. But it is also conceivable that labour may *voluntarily* withdraw itself from the market if the level of welfare payments to the unemployed is such that the incentive to find a job is materially weakened. If this happens to any great extent, it makes the official unemployment statistics an unreliable indicator of the real balance between supply and demand in the labour market.

Since 1972 the monthly figures issued by the Department of Employment have been persistently criticized because, it is said, they exaggerate the real level of unemployment in the economy. There are, in fact, two distinct strands to this argument. Firstly, the total figure of registered unemployment is said to be misleading because it lumps together groups of people whose prospects for obtaining work, and thus their length of time on the register, vary enormously. Secondly, it is argued that the figures themselves depend on the propensity of the unemployed to register and that in recent years this has been significantly increased by the provision of more generous welfare benefits. If these criticisms are valid they would obviously help to explain why, since 1966, a given level of output has been achieved with fewer workers in employment and why the stable inverse relationship which once seemed to exist between unemployment and inflation has become increasingly tenuous. Before we look at these criticisms, however, we must briefly define some of the key terms which are used in the debate.

Voluntary and involuntary unemployment

In simple terms a *voluntarily* unemployed worker is likely to be 'shopping around' for a job and may therefore have registered at the Department of Employment in order to claim benefit for the short time he expects to be out of work. Alternatively he may be quite capable of working but may have decided that his total income from social benefits and tax rebates is such that it would not be worthwhile for him to accept a job if he were offered one. By contrast a worker who is *involuntarily* unemployed is likely to be willing, even anxious, to work but unable to find a suitable job. This may be due to the fact that there are insufficient opportunities in the industry in which he has traditionally worked. His skills or experience may not be in demand or, alternatively, he may not have sufficient qualifications to get a job even though jobs are available. It follows, therefore, that an involuntarily unemployed worker is likely to be unemployed for a longer period of time than a worker who is simply between jobs.

Up to the 1930s some economists denied that prolonged involuntary unemployment could exist at all. The conventional belief was that unemployment was mainly cyclical in character. It rose and fell with the general index of industrial activity and as such was self-correcting. It was assumed that since wages and prices were free to fluctuate in response to the interplay of supply and demand, the real cost of employing labour would tend to fall at the trough of a cyclical downswing. At a lower real supply cost, entrepreneurs would tend to recruit more labour and as the next upswing got under way the economy would move nearer to full employment. It followed from this argument that anything which prevented wage rates from responding to the downward pressure of the market (such as trade unionism) was likely to impede the restoration of full employment. The only kind of non-cyclical unemployment which could arise was either *frictional*, which occurred when workers who decided to change their jobs were unable to find new work immediately, or *seasonal*, which affected those workers whose jobs depended on climatic factors.

Even in the pre-Keynesian era this view of unemployment would have been regarded by other economists as unduly simplistic. William Beveridge, Liberal social reformer and subsequent architect of our social security system, certainly recognized that *structural* unemployment was an inherent feature of industrial life:

Changes of industrial structure are constantly occurring and constantly throwing men out of employment. The very life and growth of industry consist in the replacement of old machines by new; of established processes by better ones; of labour in one form and combination by labour in fresh forms or fresh combinations. The demand for labour is thus in a state of perpetual flux and reconstruction both as to quality and as to quantity. Men who for years have satisfied the demand in one form may find the form suddenly changed; their niche in industry broken up; their hard-won skill superfluous unless they will and can learn fresh arts and find the way into unfamiliar occupations. They are displaced by economic forces entirely beyond their control and taking little or no account of personal merits.[1]

Beveridge shared with most of his contemporaries the belief that all forms of unemployment were in some measure inevitable because the demand for labour was bound 'in certain times and places to fall out of perfect adjustment to the supply'.[2] This was, of course, entirely consistent with the view, also expressed by Beveridge, that the economic system was essentially self-correcting and that public policy should therefore concentrate on improving the quality of life for those who found themselves unemployed.

The experience of the inter-war years, however, cast serious doubt on this fundamentally optimistic belief. During the 1920s a hard core of nearly one million unemployed emerged and persisted even through the modest cyclical upswings of that decade. The fact that much of this hard core was concentrated in the old staple export industries such as coal-mining, shipbuilding and cotton, and in those areas and regions which were heavily dependent on these industries, implied that the problem was structural in character. The new consumer-goods industries were generally located outside these depressed areas and were still too small to absorb the slack in the labour market.[3] Opinion in Whitehall reflected the traditional view that persistent, non-cyclical unemployment must be the result of excessive wage costs. Businessmen were not employing more labour because its price in real terms was too high. Although prices generally were tending to fall during the 1920s, money wages were 'sticky' downwards due to the short-sightedness of the trade unions. The unemployment problem could only be solved by drastic reductions in money wages – hence the prolonged confrontations between employers and trade unions in the old staple industries, culminating in the General Strike.

This simplistic view began to look even more inappropriate in the years after 1929, when severe cyclical unemployment was added to the existing structural imbalance in the labour market. Unemployment in Britain rose from 10 per cent in 1929 to 22 per cent in 1932. Other countries, notably Germany and the USA, experienced even higher rates. The expected recovery from the trough of the cycle in 1932–3 was very slow to develop and even then had only modest effects on unemployment. One symptom of the seriousness of the dislocation was the growth of long-term unemployment. In 1929 less than 5 per cent of the applicants for unemployment benefit had been unemployed for more than twelve months, but by 1936 about 25 per cent of applicants fell into this category. In certain areas the proportion was much higher and did not fall significantly even during the recovery of the late 1930s.[4] The old optimism about the ability of the economic system to right itself disappeared. Beveridge, for example, revised his earlier thinking and forecast that unemployment would continue to fluctuate between 12 per cent and 18 per cent of the insured population compared with the long-term average of $4\frac{1}{2}$ per cent before 1914.[5]

Why was the economy so sluggish near the trough of the cycle? Had full employment really gone for good? It was these questions to which J. M. Keynes addressed himself in *The*

General Theory of Employment, Interest and Money (1936). He attributed the persistence of high unemployment to a deficiency in aggregate *demand*. The level of demand was held to be dependent on consumption and investment, and if these two variables did not add up to full employment the government could fill the gap either by reducing taxation or by spending more itself. Keynes accepted the orthodox view that if full employment was to be achieved, real wages would have to be brought down to their market-clearing level, but argued that this would not be achieved through reductions in *money* wages. Instead he maintained that in a situation of high unemployment, an expansion in aggregate demand would push up prices relative to money wages and in this way would restore the labour market to full employment. As Milton Friedman has pointed out:

. . . the whole Keynesian argument for the possibility of a full employment policy arose out of the supposition that it was possible to get workers . . . to accept lower real wages produced by inflation that they would not have accepted in the direct form of a reduction in nominal wages.[6]

The main departure from traditional thinking was Keynes's insistence that unemployment might be largely *involuntary* in character and, as such, removable only through government action on the level of demand.

In the light of the *General Theory*, a critical distinction may be drawn between demand-deficient and non-demand-deficient unemployment. Both frictional and structural unemployment can either rise or fall regardless of the level of demand. As an economy moves nearer to full employment in the course of a cyclical upswing, one would expect frictional unemployment to increase as more workers find themselves in a position to choose between more and better job opportunities.[7] If, however, the demand for labour (measured, say, by the number of unfilled vacancies) rises faster than unemployment falls, it would be reasonable to assume that a significant proportion of the unemployed do not possess the skills, experience or other characteristics required by those employers who are looking for more labour. If this structural mismatch can be measured, it will give the authorities a good indication of the need for measures designed to improve labour mobility and increase the total stock of available skills, irrespective of the level of demand. Unfortuntaely the statistical data at our disposal does not enable us to quantify this structural component. Nor is the introduction of a time dimension much help, since long-term unemployment may in practice be the result either of structural imbalances or a long period of deficient demand. But if long-term unemployment shows a tendency to rise irrespective of the trend in aggregate unemployment, this may well be a clear indication that the structural component is increasing.

The use of a time dimension is the only means we have of measuring either voluntary or involuntary unemployment and it is a highly imperfect yardstick. By no means all short-term unemployment is voluntary and all long-term unemployment is not necessarily involuntary. Can a worker who is made redundant and spends, say, three weeks on the unemployment register before finding another job be described as voluntarily unemployed? Can a worker who has decided to stay on the register only until it is no longer financially worthwhile to do so (after, say, one year) be described as involuntarily unemployed? It is necessary to bear the problem of measurement in mind when discussing the various criticisms which have been made of the official statistics.

Lies and damn'd lies

The unemployment statistics cover all those unemployed persons who are registered as seeking employment and are classified by the staff of the Department of Employment offices as being capable of and available for work, whether they are entitled to unemployment benefit or not. On a certain day in every month, each employment office submits a count of all those who happen to be on the register on that particular day, which when added together make up the total unemployment figure.

Two points, however, must be stressed at the outset. Firstly, the idea that those on the register constitute a large, stagnant pool of unemployed is, as the Department itself points out, 'highly erroneous'.[8] The turnover of the register is very large. In 1975–8, for example, between 350,000 and 400,000 men and women joined or re-joined the register *every month* and a similar number left it. The difference between the inflow and outflow figures, taken in conjunction with the corresponding turnover of vacancies, gives a rough-and-ready indication of the direction in which the labour market as a whole is moving. The time spent on the register ranges from less than a day to well over two years, but the estimated *average* length of a completed spell on the register in recent years has varied between 11 and 21 weeks. In the late 1960s the average length was about 8 weeks.[9] But it should be remembered that some of the unemployed stay on the register for long, continuous periods, while others may in the course of a year register several times for short periods. The monthly count is only a snapshot of a continuously changing situation.

Secondly, the Department also points out that at any given time the number of people on the register is *not* the total number seeking work. Many people find jobs for themselves without registering as unemployed, just as employers may advertise and fill vacancies without going through their local employment office. Estimates of the number of unregistered unemployed have been made from the Census of Population in 1971 and from the General Household Surveys which suggest that in 1971–6 there were on average some 245,000 people in this category, most of them women.[10] It is thought that during the 1960s the number of unregistered unemployed women increased. Since 1971 the trend has been in the opposite direction as more married women have joined the labour market and have tended to go on the register when unemployed. The incentive for anyone to register is obviously determined by their eligibility for benefit and their wish to claim it. If, therefore, the eligibility criteria are widened and the level of benefit is improved, one would expect the number of registered unemployed to increase.

From what has already been said it must be apparent that the statistics gathered from the monthly count are open to genuine misinterpretation by anyone who wishes to discover what is really happening in local labour markets. They are also open to deliberate exploitation for political purposes. In a parliamentary debate on the economy in July 1978, for example, Mr Barney

Hayhoe, a Conservative spokesman on employment, chose to dramatize the latest monthly count in a most interesting way: 'The latest figure is 1,585,811. That means that for every hour that this Government has been in power 25 extra people have been added on average to the numbers of the unemployed: 25 for every hour, 600 for every day.' To the layman this statement might seem to suggest that the monthly figure represented a steadily rising mountain of people who had joined the unemployment register since 1974 and stayed there. Such an interpretation would, for the reasons given above, be totally misleading. The July figure is always distorted by a sudden influx of school-leavers and so the Department of Employment also issues seasonally adjusted figures. In July 1978 the seasonally adjusted total was 1,310,000. The trend in adult unemployment was quite clearly *falling* (by about 8,000 a month between September 1977 and July 1978) while notified vacancies were on a definite upward trend. Those who had been out of work for more than one year probably amounted to little more than a fifth of the total number on the register. Mr Hayhoe's interpretation of the statistics would certainly not accord with that of his colleague Sir Keith Joseph, who has repeatedly insisted that the monthly total should be disaggregated.

The monthly count is open to misinterpretation, accidental or otherwise, simply because it is far too indiscriminate a method of assessing the real level of demand for labour and lumps together different groups of people with quite different employment prospects. Thus, in order to develop a 'strategic' measure of unemployment which in his view will be much more useful to policy-makers, John Wood, with the backing of the Institute for Economic Affairs, has removed 'several irrelevant layers' from the official figures. These layers include men who are either under 25 or over 55 years of age, all men who are unemployed for less than six months and all women, adult students and occupational pensioners. Not surprisingly the effect of these removals on the overall unemployment figure is drastic. In July 1975, for example, when the official tally on the register was 1,030,000, Wood's 'strategic' indicator suggests that the 'real' figure for policy-making purposes was a mere 116,000.

Are these revisions justified? Wood seeks to exclude *school-leavers* from the overall figure on the grounds that they are simply a temporary distortion:

Many young people take time to find a first job, and understandably even longer to find one that is suitable. There is a high turnover and the two or three jobs which young people often try before they settle down may be separated by brief periods on the register thus increasing the number of 'job-changers'.[11]

While the great majority of school-leavers fall into this category the evidence suggests that since 1974 the ability of the economy to absorb school-leavers has significantly diminished. There now seems to be a small but growing number of school-leavers who are not able to find a job of any kind, still less to 'shop around' in the manner described by Wood, and thus remain on the register for several months after the normal peak in school-leaver unemployment in July and August (see Table 1).

Table 1

Unemployed school-leavers in Great Britain (thousands)

	August		December	
1969	35·8	(2·4)	2·9	(2·4)
1970	36·3	(2·6)	3·8	(2·6)
1971	55·5	(3·6)	8·6	(3·8)
1972	60·9	(3·8)	9·7	(3·3)
1973	21·6	(2·5)	1·8	(2·2)
1974	56·0	(2·8)	8·0	(2·7)*
1975	158·2	(4·8)	32·0	(5·0)
1976	194·5	(6·2)	48·0	(5·6)
1977	220·4	(6·7)	54·3	(6·1)

Source: *Department of Employment Gazette*, various issues. Figures in parenthesis indicate the percentage rate of unemployment for Great Britain; *November 1974.

The argument against considering school-leavers as un-employed in the normal sense rests on the assumption that nothing useful can be learned from them about the real balance between supply and demand in the labour market. This is surely a mistake. The significant deterioration in the employment position of this group in 1975–7 may, of course, simply reflect the exceptional circumstances of the recession. But in so far as there has been a permanent loss of job opportunities for school-leavers, a nascent structural problem may be involved. This possibility is discussed in Chapter Three. In any case Wood argues for the exclusion not only of school-leavers but of all those aged between 16 and 25. Presumably he feels that the unemployment problem in this age group is largely frictional in character and may thus be disregarded. There is no evidence, however, to support this view. Most people who have been on the register for more than six months cannot be said to be frictionally unemployed and in January 1978 about 30 per cent of all those in the 18–25 age group had been unemployed for more than six months.[12]

A more radical proposal advanced by Wood and several others is that *all frictionally unemployed workers* should be excluded from the total figure. The rationale of this argument is that a clear distinction must be drawn between simple job-changing and 'real' unemployment:

Changing jobs is a desirable process both for the individual and for society. Most people want to improve their position, and in so far as moves take place from lower to higher productivity occupations, society gains. Indeed, there is no other way in which an economy can adapt itself to the future. As new tastes and new preferences develop, old jobs disappear and new ones take their place. In the process some people must leave one job to find another. In so doing many may register for new work and appear as unemployed, even though they rapidly find new work.[13]

Frictional unemployment, in short, is viewed as being largely voluntary and relatively costless. Yet, in practice, the disappearance of many 'old jobs' has been achieved only through enforced redundancy. In 1966, for example, the Wilson government introduced a package of deflationary measures, the avowed intention of which was to force employers to 'shake out' underemployed labour. It was anticipated that much of this labour would be redeployed in export industries and that the process of redeployment would be greatly eased by redundancy payments, wage-related unemployment benefits and retraining. But the shake-out did not have such a desirable effect. A survey by Mackay of redundancies in West Midlands engineering plants found that most of those workers who lost their jobs were relatively elderly, had no marketable skills, and (in the case of men) often experienced long spells of unemployment after the shake-out. Many of those who did find other jobs were obliged to move into the service sector.[14] It is therefore unwise to assume that most frictionally unemployed workers are in the process of moving to higher productivity jobs. The ability of redundant workers to obtain new jobs depends on their age, experience, and qualifications, and on the availability of *suitable* alternative employment opportunities. To the extent that employers use redundancy payments in order to shake out relatively marginal workers, they will simply be contributing to the problem of long-term unemployment.

Another questionable assumption in Wood's argument is that frictional unemployment can be equated with all unemployment which lasts for no more than eight weeks. If this arbitrary cut-off point had been applied to the total level of registered unemployment in, say, 1976 it would have reduced the aggregate figure by nearly one-third. The crude statistics on duration of unemployment are an extremely unreliable index of frictional unemployment. These statistics are derived from the monthly count of those who are on the register on a particular day and as such give no information on *completed* spells of unemployment. It seems highly probable, therefore, that many of those who are recorded as having been unemployed for less than two months in a particular count will remain out of work for some period in excess of two months. The available evidence (summarized in Table 2) suggests that the expected duration of unemployment varies directly with the overall level of unemployment, and that frictional unemployment varies inversely with this level.[15]

Consequently it might be expected that in periods of relatively high unemployment, a simple application of the 'two month' criterion would greatly exaggerate the real level of frictional unemployment. This expectation has been confirmed by Hughes's analysis of vacancy statistics, which concludes that in the relatively bad year of 1972 those who were frictionally unemployed amounted to little more than 40 per cent of those who at the monthly count were shown as having been unemployed for less

Table 2
Unemployment by duration, 1959–77

Percentage of total number unemployed

	Less than 8 weeks	Over 8 and up to 26 weeks	Over 26 and up to 52 weeks	Over 52 weeks	Overall rate (%)
—1950	58·2	19·1	9·6	13·1	1·5
—1955	63·0	16·2	8·7	12·1	1·1
—1960	48·9	20·0	12·2	18·9	1·6
—1965	52·0	21·1	10·2	16·8	1·4
—1970	45·1	24·9	12·2	17·7	2·5
1971	41·7	29·2	13·3	15·8	3·6
1972	36·3	27·3	14·4	22·0	3·5
1973	38·5	21·8	12·0	27·6	2·2
1974	42·4	25·6	11·6	20·5	2·7
—1975	38·7	32·6	14·1	14·7	4·8
1976	31·5	31·4	17·1	20·0	5·7
1977	29·6	32·3	16·0	22·3	6·2

Source: British Labour Statistics, 1971 and 1973; *Department of Employment Gazette*, 1978. Figures relate to October of each year, except 1950, 1955 and 1960 when the September figure has been used.

than two months.[16] While all frictional unemployment must by definition be of short duration, all short-term unemployment is not frictional and cannot therefore be used to justify arbitrary revisions of the aggregate unemployment figures.

Another group which, according to Wood, should be excluded from the official figures is that which comprises people who are virtually *unemployable*. Indeed he has asserted that in periods of high demand for labour as many as half the total number of men on the register 'are unfit for normal work'.[17] This conclusion is arrived at by taking the results of the Department of Employment's own investigations into the characteristics of the unemployed in 1961, 1964 and 1973 – all years of relatively low unemployment – and assuming that those who were thought by the Department to have poor prospects of obtaining work and/or were 'somewhat unenthusiastic' about their attitude to work would not be able to hold down a job even if they were offered one. But the Department has warned against reading too much into these surveys:

There is no doubt that the register includes some people who might be described as 'unemployable', who are exceptionally difficult to place and who seldom hold down a job for more than a week or two. These tend to be found among the elderly, unskilled or socially disadvantaged, and people who find it difficult to adapt to the conditions of working life. However, although some individuals are clearly more employable than others, it is not possible to draw a clear line.[18]

A more recent survey by the Department in 1976 reported that 24 per cent of men and 13 per cent of women on the register had poor prospects *and* were somewhat unenthusiastic in their attitude to work, compared with 31 per cent and 22 per cent respectively in 1973.[19] Following the logic of Wood's argument one would therefore deduct 143,000 from the monthly total of 477,000 unemployed (excluding school-leavers) in June 1973, and from the total of 994,000 recorded in June 1976 one would deduct 213,000. Yet for such a deduction to be valid it must surely be established that those in this category would refuse a job even if they were offered one. In reality, such a refusal would risk the loss of unemployment benefit, while the Department's own evidence suggests that *some* people in this category are offered and accept jobs.[20] To exclude all those who are judged to have 'poor prospects' of obtaining work, irrespective of whether they are keen to find work or not, is even more dubious. In June 1976 some 412,000 people (including the 'unenthusiastic' group mentioned above) fell into this category, compared with 278,000 in June 1973. But as Hughes has pointed out, the number who are assessed as having poor prospects of securing a long-term job will vary directly with the overall level of unemployment.[21] To exclude this number from the overall figure is surely, therefore, to engage in a self-fulfilling prophecy:

As unemployment rises, those groups most at risk, such as the elderly, have less chance of obtaining work. Because they have little chance of obtaining work the critics argue that they should be excluded from the numbers of unemployed. But most people would consider that not being able to obtain work is what unemployment is all about.[22]

The longer these people are out of work, the less enthusiastic they may become about the whole idea of getting work.

30

The final major revision for which Wood argues involves the complete removal of the statistics on female unemployment from the total. The rationale behind this proposal is that the labour market for women is quite distinct from the market for men. Wood points out that since 1966 male employment has been falling while female employment has been rising. Female unemployment, he maintains, also 'displays quite different characteristics (from male), and is on a much smaller scale'. Long-term unemployment among women is, he argues, virtually non-existent.[23] In 1974–7, however, the differences between male and female unemployment rates became rather less marked. Although the number of jobs for men continued to decline, female employment remained virtually static. Female *unemployment*, however, rose because more married women entered the labour market in search of work. In April 1977, for example, 26 per cent of the total number of registered unemployed were women, compared with 16 per cent in April 1974. Similarly the ratio of men to women on the register fell from 5:1 in April 1973 to 2·6:1 in April 1978. Long-term unemployment among women has also become more significant. In April 1975, for example, only 14·9 per cent of women on the register had been unemployed for more than six months, compared with 30·0 per cent of men. By April 1978 these proportions had risen to 38·2 per cent and 46·9 per cent respectively. These figures suggest that trends in the two labour markets have begun to converge. Whether this convergence will continue remains to be seen, but it hardly supports the case for a complete separation of males and females for the purpose of computing the overall level of unemployment.

Two other relatively minor groups included in the monthly count should be mentioned. It has occasionally been argued that fraudulent claimants for unemployment benefit have a distorting effect on the figures. Bourlet and Bell estimated that as many as 130,000 people were fraudulent claimants (and therefore wrongly on the register) in January 1972 and Wood quoted a figure of 100,000 for December 1971.[24] The Department of Employment's own investigations, however, suggest that in 1973 only 2·9 per cent of unemployed workers in receipt of benefit were making fraudulent claims.[25] Wood subsequently revised his own figure to a more modest 'guesstimate' of about 10,000, and the real incidence of fraud is unlikely to be greatly in excess of this level. The second group comprises those who retire prematurely with an occupational pension and register as unemployed simply in order to qualify for a full state pension when they reach the age of 65. Estimates of those in this category vary, but they are unlikely to be in excess of 30,000.[26]

No serious student of the subject would seek to claim that the official unemployment statistics could not be made more relevant to the needs of policy-makers. As Hughes has pointed out, total unemployment must be broken down into its various components, particularly frictional, structural and demand-deficient, before it can furnish us with really meaningful information about what is going on in labour markets. To do this, we need more frequent and detailed surveys of the characteristics of the unemployed, and much more information about completed spells of unemployment. But the solution to the problem of interpreting the official figures does *not* lie in making arbitrary revisions of the kind proposed by Wood.

A more productive line of inquiry is to accept that over the past decade or so there has been a significant increase in registered unemployment and then to ask why this has happened. How much of this increase is due to deficient demand and how much of it reflects non-demand factors? It has already been suggested that the level of unemployment for a given pressure of demand has risen. This could reflect either a growing mismatch between the unemployed and the jobs that are available or a change in the supply of labour. A 'supply shift' could in theory have been brought about by the provision of enhanced welfare benefits to the unemployed since the mid-1960s. The availability of these benefits may have encouraged more workers to change their jobs and spend more time 'shopping around' the market. It may also have induced more unemployed workers to go on the register in order to claim benefit. If a 'supply shift' has in fact occurred, it would imply an increase in voluntary unemployment and would rule out the application of conventional Keynesian remedies.

Sturdy beggars

In recent years the feeling has grown that many of those who are unemployed have consciously chosen to be so. The availability of enhanced welfare benefits has, it is argued, broken the link between unemployment and poverty and has therefore made nonsense of the official statistics as a guide to the real level of demand for labour. Commenting on the Heath government's political sensitivity to rising unemployment in 1971 and on the consequent reversal of its economic strategy, Ralph Harris, of the Institute for Economic Affairs, has argued that

The government might have resisted the stampede by pondering the reassuring press report of the latter-day Jarrow 'marchers' who joined a demonstration in London after travelling down comfortably by Pullman train . . . it made . . . the error of failing to grasp the deceptive nature of the official statistics as a measure of the absolute level of 'unemployment', let alone as a measure of social distress in an age of wage-related benefits and prompt tax repayments.[27]

Advocates of the 'sturdy beggar' thesis usually point out that the introduction of statutory redundancy payments and the Earnings-Related Supplement in 1965–6 was followed by a rapid and apparently permanent rise in unemployment. They also draw attention to a radical change in the relationship between unemployment and vacancies which began in 1966 and has continued up to the present time. Up to 1966 unemployment was low when vacancies were high and vice versa; since 1966 a given level of vacancies has been associated with higher and higher levels of unemployment. In 1975, for example, the level of vacancies was roughly the same as in 1967 yet unemployment was nearly twice as high.[28] Does this new relationship not indicate that many unemployed workers must be spending more time 'shopping around' for suitable jobs, aided by generous welfare benefits?

In answering this question we must note that the effects of the Redundancy Payments Act of 1965 on both the level and duration of unemployment have been greatly exaggerated. Firstly, fewer than half of those who are made redundant actually receive any statutory compensation. In Daniel's detailed sample, only 7 per cent had received payments under the Act and these workers tended to be in the higher occupational groups. While those who received 'substantial lump sums' were less anxious to find a new job, so few people fell into this category that the effect on the overall level of unemployment must have been extremely marginal.[29] Secondly, the *average* payment made is not of such a size as would deter most workers from actively seeking another job. In 1975, for example, slightly over 340,000 workers received £178 million in redundancy payments, which amounts to about £500 per worker. A direct study of the effects of the Act made in 1969 by the OPCS found that redundancy payments had helped only a small minority of workers to find better jobs than they might otherwise have done.[30] Other research has confirmed these general conclusions.[31] Thirdly, the Act does not discriminate between those with good prospects of getting alternative employment and those who, by contrast, are likely to be out of work for some considerable time. Some employees are able to start a new job almost immediately while others are much less fortunate. The size of a redundancy payment is determined by the earnings, age and length of service of the individual employee. Although some elderly workers, for example, may pick up relatively large payments, it is their age rather than the payments themselves which is likely to delay their re-entry into the labour market.

The contribution of Earnings-Related Supplement (ERS) to the level and duration of unemployment may be more significant. ERS is payable to those who are already receiving the flat-rate unemployment benefit and who have been unemployed for at least twelve working days. Entitlement to ERS expires after six months, but it *could* encourage workers to stay on the register for this length of time. The proportion of all recipients of unemployment benefit entitled to claim ERS rose from 26 per cent in 1966 to about 40 per cent in 1976, although many of those in receipt of ERS would still have been unemployed in the absence of this benefit. Nevertheless it must also be remembered that for a married man on average earnings with two children, the level of benefit rose from 49 per cent of his after-tax earnings in 1965 to 73 per cent in 1967. Evans, for example, has argued that the change in the unemployment-vacancy relationship which occurred in the mid-1960s can be attributed in part to an increased propensity to register by unemployed men, which was in turn due to the introduction of ERS.[32] Maki and Spindler have reached a broadly similar conclusion, although they also point out that 'a large part of the post-1966 change in unemployment experience may be due to an increase in the rate of technical progress which has affected the efficiency of the labour force'.[33] It is clearly very difficult to quantify any *autonomous* effect which ERS may have had on the unemployment rate after the mid-1960s. We may, however, note that since 1967 the size of this benefit relative to net earnings has not increased, so that if ERS had a significant effect on the level of registered unemployment it may only have been a once-for-all increase in 1966–7.[34]

Increases in the standard level of social security benefits may also have prolonged the duration of unemployment, but the evidence is generally inconclusive. It is certainly true, as Brittan has pointed out, that the supplementary benefit level for a three-child family rose significantly in relation to the average net earnings of male manual workers between the late 1950s and the late 1960s.[35] Yet between 1967 and 1977 the level of unemployment increased by a factor of three without any further improvement in the benefit-earnings relationship. In April 1976 the ratio of flat-rate and earnings-related benefits to disposable earnings for a married couple with two children was, at 65 per cent, almost exactly the same as in 1967. At no time between 1971 and 1976 did the benefit-earnings ratio exceed 67 per cent.[36]

Some people will, of course, do better and some worse than the average figure quoted above suggests. It must also be remembered that the increasing number of manual workers who have crossed the threshold of PAYE over the last decade means that many more of those becoming unemployed receive tax rebates. The question which must be answered is whether the total level of benefit and rebate available to individuals is likely to prolong their search for another job or weaken their motivation to work at all. Those in receipt of the least benefit are young men without any dependents, and it is precisely this group who are most likely to engage in extensive job-swapping. It could be argued, however, that a high level of job mobility is an inherent characteristic of the under-25 age group which would not be seriously affected even if the level of benefit available to this group were increased. At the other end of the scale are those married men who have several children and who, if they were in work, would have low-paid jobs. For unemployed men the level of benefit rises with the number of their dependents. Those with four or more children, earning a weekly wage within the short range of income in which means-tested benefits are withdrawn (the 'poverty trap'), are likely to be better off unemployed than they would be in work. It is therefore quite reasonable to suggest that men who have a relatively large number of dependents *and whose prospects of getting work are poor* may well take much longer to find jobs once they are on the register. In the words of one study carried out by Political and Economic Planning (PEP) in 1976, 'These higher benefits lead men to have a higher asking price for working. When what they have to sell to an employer is worth no more than their counterparts whose benefit and asking price are lower, then they take longer to find jobs.' It must be emphasized, however, that men in this category tended to be unskilled and physically unfit for work and would at a time of rising unemployment find it increasingly difficult to obtain work in any case. As PEP concluded: '. . . the more children men had, the more they tended to be unfit and low-skilled. Child dependency allowances, it seems, led men to seek higher levels of pay and consequently to be out of work longer.'[37]

It is the familiar conjunction of low pay, low tax-thresholds and dependency-related benefits which explains why about 10 per cent of those on the unemployment register are as well off or better off 'on the dole' than they would be in work. To the extent that the benefit-earnings ratio encourages them to stay on the register, one can describe them as voluntarily unemployed. But if the 'sturdy beggar' hypothesis is to have any validity as an explanation of the upward trend in *total* unemployment, it must surely be necessary to show that the level of benefit is keeping on the register men who would otherwise be able to obtain jobs without undue difficulty. In the case of the minority who are better off unemployed, one may well be dealing with a group of men for whom it would in any case be difficult to find employment, particularly during economic recessions. If the level of dependency-benefit were reduced it must be doubted whether the increased financial motivation to work would be sufficient to counteract the disadvantages which many of those who receive most benefit would encounter in a competitive labour market. Thus, in his 1973 study, Daniel concluded that:

Where unemployed workers had little or no interest in finding a job this was generally because they were approaching retirement age, because of their level of fitness or state of health, because of their family or domestic circumstances, or because they had little or no chance of finding a job, and certainly not because of the level of social benefit received. Where, however, the worker was marginal for one of the social, demographic or physical reasons listed, then the level of benefit received was inclined to have an influence.[38]

The 'sturdy beggar' hypothesis assumes that a large proportion of the unemployed have chosen to remain on the register after a rational calculation of the financial costs and benefits involved. Having made that calculation, and decided that for them continued unemployment is eminently rational, they are quite happy to be 'welfare parasites'. While this may indeed be true of certain individuals – principally those men with large families who would be receiving less income if they were in work – it seems highly implausible as a *general* explanation of the increasing level and duration of unemployment. We must also take into account those investigations which show that for most men the experience of unemployment is sufficiently unpleasant for them not to prolong it voluntarily. Except for those in the marginal categories discussed above, Daniel found that many of those who were receiving relatively high levels of benefit (and thus had family commitments) were the *most* anxious to find another job. Nearly three-quarters of those in his survey, for example, said that it had been 'bad' or 'very bad' for them personally to be out of work. The minority who took a different view were largely those who had reconciled themselves to the idea of being unemployed. Lack of money was the factor most frequently mentioned by the majority, but psychological costs (such as boredom) and social costs (such as a sense of losing status) were also felt to be important.[39] Other studies have underlined the point that for most people enthusiasm to get another job and, equally important, confidence that they *can* get another job both tend to decline the longer they are unemployed. The experience of prolonged unemployment seems to undermine the motivation to work. Research suggests that the biggest psychological shock comes when the individual realizes that his unemployment may not be a passing phase but could last several months or even years.[40] In short, the theory that a large proportion of the unemployed consciously choose to be out of work for longer than they would be if welfare benefits were less generous is not supported by the available evidence.

Summary

The fundamental question posed by the critics is whether or not the unemployment trends recorded by the official statistics have been a misleading guide to policy-makers. The burden of their argument is that these statistics greatly exaggerate the level of unemployment which can be regarded as involuntary and demand-deficient in the Keynesian sense. Increases in the level of welfare benefits since 1966 have allegedly encouraged more people to change their jobs and to spend more time 'shopping around' the market. The official statistics, however, have concealed this underlying trend and prompted policy-makers to over-stimulate demand, with disastrous consequences for the rate of inflation and the balance of payments. Consequently the official figures must be re-interpreted in a way which will reveal the 'true' level of involuntary unemployment. This means that groups such as school-leavers, the unemployable, the 'sturdy beggars', and all the short-term unemployed should be excluded from the aggregate figure.

The critics are undoubtedly correct in pointing out the dangers involved in a return to the crude, pseudo-Keynesian reflationary strategy adopted by the Heath government in 1972–3. But their attempts to explain away the current level of unemployment by 'revising' the statistics are unconvincing. Even if a clear distinction could be drawn between voluntary and involuntary unemployment, it by no means follows that all short-term unemployment is necessarily voluntary. Nor is it possible to quantify how many people on the register are permanently unemployable. While there will always be a significant number of people who, even in the tightest market, find it very difficult to get a job and keep it, the evidence suggests that this number will fluctuate with the overall level of demand. School-leavers are in fact excluded from the adjusted aggregate figures issued by the Department of Employment so that the question of policy-makers being misled does not arise in their case. The current trend in unemployment among school-leavers, however, can hardly be ignored. The critics have a more plausible case for excluding the 'sturdy beggars' from the aggregate figures but this would reduce the overall total by no more than 10 per cent. In any case there is no evidence to suggest that as a proportion of the total number of unemployed this group has increased significantly in recent years, whatever may have happened in the mid-1960s.

This does not, of course, mean that changes in the supply schedule of labour can be entirely discounted. The effect of statutory redundancy payments, tax rebates, ERS and other social benefits may well have been to prolong periods of job search and thus to enlarge the aggregate unemployment figure recorded at each monthly count. There is, however, a major difficulty in isolating the contribution of supply shifts to the volume of unemployment. If, for example, the unemployed are taking longer to find other jobs, does this simply mean that they can afford to take longer, or does it mean that there are fewer jobs on offer? If the level of unemployment has increased relative to a given number of vacancies, does this imply that the unemployed have become more choosy, or does it rather suggest that the competition for available jobs has increased? Did the introduction of ERS and redundancy payments in 1966 lead directly to the shake-out of labour which began in that year, or was this really caused by the sharp downturn in demand, coupled with faster productivity growth? None of these questions can be answered conclusively; the existing evidence only allows us to form judgements based on the balance of probabilities. In the course of this chapter we have sought to show that changes on the supply side do not seem to have played the dominant role. Our attention must therefore move to those factors which have influenced the level of demand in the labour market.

CHAPTER THREE

Particular People, Particular Places

> Men may come to lose their former qualifications through
> an objective change in the methods of production. Men
> may gradually lose their former qualifications through the
> subjective change brought by advancing years. Men may
> from the beginning lack industrial qualifications through
> deficiencies of industrial training. There is thus opened a
> wide field for maladjustment of quality between supply and
> demand. The narrowing of that field must depend mainly
> upon the possibility of spreading more accurate informa-
> tion as to the character of the demand from time to time,
> and of securing the mobility and adaptability of the
> supply.
>
> W. H. Beveridge, 1909

Since the mid-1960s there has been a clear tendency for unemployment to rise independently of the general level of demand in the
economy. If this trend cannot be primarily attributed to a benefit-
induced growth in voluntary unemployment, we must consider
the possibility that the characteristics of those looking for work
are becoming increasingly mismatched with the kind of jobs
available.

The 'mismatch' or structural hypothesis is often applied to the
American pattern of unemployment, and some observers feel
that Britain has in recent years been moving towards this pattern.
The upward trend in American unemployment since 1970 has
affected some groups far more than others. Black workers, male
and female alike, are twice as likely to be unemployed as whites.
The under-20 age group has also been disproportionately affected,
but the unemployment rate among black teenagers (33 per cent
in 1974 and rising) was more than twice that among young whites.
Employment opportunities for black male youths have actually
been declining since the late 1960s. Meanwhile more and more

41

white married women have entered the labour market and now constitute over 40 per cent of the labour force. Simultaneously those in the 'prime' working group (white males between 25 and 45 years of age) have fallen to only about 20 per cent of the labour force. Some economists have concluded, therefore, that the relatively low attractiveness of the majority of workers, the fact that employers regard many of them as undesirable and unproductive, explains the rising trend of unemployment in the USA. Does this analysis have any relevance to Britain's current problem? A brief analysis of the changing structure of employment and the characteristics of the unemployed throws further light on this question.

The labour force and employment

The supply of labour is determined firstly by the rate of population growth and secondly by the proportion of the adult population which is either working or looking for work (the 'activity rate'). Throughout Western Europe there was a marked increase in national birth rates during the early 1960s, resulting in a relatively heavy flow of young people into the labour market during the mid-1970s. In Britain this demographic trend began in 1955 and lasted until 1964, so that from 1970 onwards there was a significant increase in the number of school-leavers. In 1969–70 some 691,000 young people left school; by 1975–6 this figure had risen to 817,000. This would not have mattered so much if there had been a corresponding growth in the proportion of young people going into further full-time education, but this did not happen.[1] Thus the number of school-leavers immediately available for work rose from 500,000 in July 1970 to 637,000 in July 1976. Simultaneously there was a rapid increase in the activity rate of married women which brought an extra one million of them into the labour market between 1971 and 1976. It is believed that the movement towards equal pay and the increased opportunities for part-time work in the service sector have encouraged more women to seek employment. Whatever the reason, the female working population steadily increased between 1971 and 1976 while the number of females in employment showed a corresponding increase until 1976 when there was a slight fall. By contrast, the male working population remained virtually static during this period and after 1974 male employment declined. These trends are summarized in Table 3.

Table 3

Comparison of working population and labour force estimates (thousands)

Working population

	1971	1972	1973	1974	1975	1976
Employees in employment						
Males	13,424	13,319	13,478	13,363	13,240	13,052
Females	8,224	8,331	8,705	8,933	8,973	8,945
Total	21,648	21,650	22,182	22,297	22,218	21,997
Employers and self-employed						
Males	1,471	1,464	1,513	1,493	1,456	1,456
Females	371	371	371	371	369	369
Total	1,842	8,835	1,884	1,864	1,825	1,825
HM Forces						
Males	353	356	346	331	322	321
Females	15	15	15	14	15	15
Total	368	371	361	345	336	336
Employed labour force						
Males	15,248	15,139	15,337	15,187	15,018	14,829
Females	8,610	8,717	9,091	9,318	9,357	9,329
Total	23,858	23,856	24,427	24,506	24,374	24,158
Registered unemployed						
Males	589	647	461	439	680	972
Females	98	119	84	75	149	306
Total	687	765	545	515	828	1,278
Total working population						
Males	15,837	15,786	15,798	15,626	15,698	15,801
Females	8,708	8,836	9,175	9,393	9,506	9,635
Total	24,545	24,621	24,972	25,021	25,202	25,436

Source: *Department of Employment Gazette*, June 1977.

It has been suggested, therefore, that in 1974–6 male unemployment increased because there were fewer jobs for men, while female unemployment rose because more women were seeking work.[2]

Another side-effect of the rising activity rate of married women has been the growing tendency for those who cannot obtain work to register as unemployed. Between 1971 and 1974 females comprised, on average, about 15 per cent of the registered unemployed; by April 1977 this proportion had risen to 26 per cent. If the female propensity to register had stayed the same during the post-1974 recession this would have reduced the April 1977 figure of registered unemployed by about 120,000.

The growth of female unemployment may also reflect the recent tendency for employment in the service sector to increase more slowly than it did up to 1974 (see Table 4).

Table 4

Summary of the changing structure of employment by industry, 1971–7, Great Britain

	Employees in employment males and females (thousands)				% Change:	
	June	June	Dec.	Dec.		
Industrial sector	1971	1974	1976	1977	1971–4	1974–7
Manufacturing	7,886	7,705	7,207	7,232	−2·2	−6·1
Engineering and shipbuilding	2,184	2,129	1,989	2,002	−2·2	−5·9
Metal and metal goods	1,935	1,867	1,760	1,786	−3·5	−4·3
Other manufacturing	3,767	3,709	3,458	3,444	−1·5	−7·1
Construction	1,222	1,290	1,253	1,234	+5·5	−4·3
Services	11,357	12,214	12,653	12,698	+7·5	+3·9
Transport and communications	1,545	1,483	1,434	1,422	−4·0	−4·1
Distribution	2,555	2,707	2,724	2,728	+6·3	+0·7
Insurance, banking, finance, etc.	962	1,101	1,109	1,135	+14·4	+3·0
Professional and scientific	2,916	3,284	3,572	3,576	+12·6	+8·9
Miscellaneous services	1,906	2,088	2,226	2,264	+9·5	+8·4
Public admin. and defence	1,473	1,551	1,586	1,572	+5·3	+1·3
Other industries	1,183	1,088	1,057	1,050	−8·0	−3·4
All industries and services	21,648	22,297	22,176	22,214	+2·9	−0·3

Source: *Department of Employment Gazette*, Annual Census of Employment and Quarterly Estimates of Employees in Employment.

Table 4 also shows that manufacturing employment declined throughout the period, but that after 1974 it fell nearly three times as fast as it did before. This trend has affected employment opportunities for men much more than those for women since all the declining industries employ relatively high proportions of men. In engineering and shipbuilding, for example, men outnumber women by nearly three to one and in the metal goods sector by nearly five to one. In professional and scientific services, by contrast, women outnumber men by two to one and exceed them in every other service industry except the transport group and public administration. From a regional perspective the trend is clear and almost uniform in incidence. In the course of 1977, for example, male employment declined in every region except two (the South West and the West Midlands) where it was static. By contrast, female employment showed a slight upward trend in every region, including those with the highest rates of total unemployment.

One symptom of declining employment opportunities for men is the growth of *long-term* male unemployment. Each cyclical peak of economic activity since the mid-1950s has not only left a larger number of men unemployed than at the previous peak but has also seen a growing proportion of them out of work for more than six months.[3] This is a disturbing trend in view of the perceived tendency for individuals to lose their motivation to work as the duration of their unemployment increases. In January 1978, for example, slightly over 43 per cent of unemployed men had been on the register for more than six months, compared with 34 per cent two years earlier. If long-term unemployment is measured by the number of workers who have been on the register for more than one year, then in January 1978 there were 272,000 men in this category, or 25 per cent of all unemployed men. Were it to be shown that all these men were 'unemployable', the importance of this trend for economic policy-makers would be open to question. But a survey by the Department of Employment in June 1976 revealed that three-quarters of the increase in male and female unemployment since June 1973 had occurred among those with 'good, fair or reasonable' prospects of obtaining work.[4] This evidence might, of course, be used to support the conventional argument that the post-1974 increase in long-term unemployment is simply due to the severity of the recent recession and the prolonged stagnation of aggregate demand. A more detailed analysis of the characteristics of the unemployed, however, suggests that structural factors may also be influential.

Age and unemployment: the young

Unemployment among men is heavily concentrated in the oldest and youngest age groups. Among women, where the overall rate is much lower, unemployment is heavily concentrated in the youngest group (see Table 5).

Table 5

Estimated unemployment rates by age in Great Britain, 1975–8
(percentages)

	July 1975	January 1976	July 1976	January 1977	July 1977	January 1978
Males						
16–17	13·8	12·4	26·8	13·0	28·5	13·3
18–19	9·6	11·1	10·5	10·9	11·2	10·7
20–24	6·8	10·0	9·3	10·1	9·6	10·3
25–29	5·2	7·1	6·6	7·4	6·8	7·5
30–39	4·4	5·9	5·6	6·3	5·9	6·6
40–49	3·7	4·9	4·7	5·2	4·9	5·3
50–59	3·7	4·7	4·6	5·1	5·0	5·4
60 and over	7·8	9·5	9·5	10·3	9·5	10·2
All ages	5·4	7·0	7·3	7·3	7·7	7·6
Females						
16–17	10·5	12·0	25·8	14·3	29·7	15·6
18–19	6·1	8·0	9·0	9·7	11·0	10·6
20–24	3·0	5·3	5·9	7·0	7·6	8·3
25–29	2·1	3·0	3·4	4·1	4·3	4·9
30–39	1·0	1·5	1·8	2·1	2·3	2·6
40–49	0·9	1·2	1·4	1·7	1·8	1·9
50–59	1·3	1·7	1·9	2·1	2·2	2·4
60 and over	0·2	0·2	0·2	0·2	0·2	0·2
All ages	2·1	2·9	4·0	3·8	5·0	4·5

Source: *Department of Employment Gazette*, May 1978.

The unemployment rate in the youngest age group is of course temporarily inflated every July by the movement of school-leavers on to the register. Yet not only has the July rate increased sharply since 1968 (when it was still only 5 per cent) but, equally important, the *January* rate for school-leavers is now higher than for any other age group. The rising level of unemployment among school-leavers is not peculiar to the UK. Indeed there seems to have been a significant deterioration in the employment prospects of the 16–25 age group as a whole in many industrial countries since the late 1960s, so that the ratio of youth to adult unemployment has increased (see Table 6).

Table 6

Ratio of youth (under 25) to adult
unemployment rates, in eight
countries

	1970	1976
Belgium	N.A.	1·7
Britain	1·2	3·4
France	1·3	2·6*
West Germany	0·8	1·7
Holland	0·9	3·3
Italy	6·8	9·0
Spain	3·3	3·8
Sweden	2·2	3·0

* 1975

Source: OECD.

In 1976 in the countries within the Organization for Economic Co-operation and Development (OECD) as a whole, about 40 per cent of the unemployed were under 25, although this age group accounted for only 22 per cent of the working population.[5]

There is, of course, one very obvious reason why youth unemployment might be relatively worse during a recession. Employers who face a downturn in demand may well seek to avoid compulsory redundancies by cutting back on recruitment and allowing 'natural wastage' to reduce their labour force. Such a strategy will clearly tend to discriminate against school-leavers and young workers in general. Recent work by the Department of Employment suggests that when the unemployment rate for *all* male workers rises by one percentage point, the unemployment rate for males under 20 (excluding school-leavers) increases by about 1·7 percentage points. The same relationship has also held in upswings when overall male unemployment has fallen less quickly than male youth unemployment.[6] The cyclical sensitivity of youth employment suggests that many young workers are regarded as a marginal source of labour by firms. To the extent that this is true, it means that in a prolonged and severe recession youth unemployment is bound to show a disproportionate increase.

The cyclical movement of youth unemployment may also reflect changes in the propensity of young people to *register* as unemployed. As the Department of Employment points out:

> Young people form a high proportion of those who are unemployed for short periods, and it may be that during a boom many young people are unemployed for such short periods that they do not register as unemployed. A small increase in the average duration of unemployment during a recession may induce this group to register as unemployed with a consequent disproportionate increase in the figures of registered unemployment for young people.[7]

It must be remembered that the raising of the school-leaving age to 16 in 1972 means that school-leavers can now claim supplementary benefit immediately and this will have increased the incentive to register.

It is at least conceivable, however, that the upward trend in youth unemployment may reflect certain fundamental, longer-term changes in the demand for young people. Firstly, the relative cost of employing young workers, especially males, has increased quite sharply in recent years. The gradual implementation of the Equal Pay Act of 1970 together with the effects of flat-rate incomes policies have brought the average hourly earnings of males under 21 much closer to the adult male average.[8] Many now receive the full adult rate at 18, and to this extent their attractiveness as cheap labour has diminished. Secondly, there is some evidence, admittedly anecdotal, to suggest that many employers have become less willing to employ young people for a variety of non-financial reasons. A survey by the Manpower Services Commission (1976) found that employers are often critical of standards among school-leavers, particularly their attitude to work, their appearance and behaviour and their lack of basic education.[9] An earlier report from the Federation of Personnel Services expressed the view that many young people left school ill-equipped for any kind of job at all.[10] It is worth pointing out that in 1976-7 about 60 per cent of school-leavers in England and Wales entered the labour market at the minimum age with either very poor academic qualifications or none at all.[11] An additional factor affecting the employment prospects of young females is the growing activity rate among married women. If employers *are* becoming reluctant to recruit young people, they may as a result be tending to fill vacancies with older, relatively experienced and 'reliable' women, more and more of whom are now available.

The effects of these underlying changes in the demand for young people must also be viewed against changes on the supply side of the market. In 1966-7, for example, there were 619,000 school-leavers in England and Wales, but by 1976-7 this figure had risen to 768,000, and official projections suggest a further increase to 820,000 by 1980-81.[12] Obviously one would expect an increase in the absolute number of school-leavers to be followed by a rise in the absolute number of young unemployed. But if a demographic increase occurs against a background of static or falling employment opportunities, there will be a rise in the *rate* of youth unemployment. In Britain as in the USA certain geographical areas (for example, inner cities) have experienced exceptionally high rates of youth unemployment since 1974, which must obviously be related to the structure of local employment. The longer-term prospects facing the unskilled and unqualified young people who live in these areas seem increasingly bleak.

Age and unemployment: the old

While recognizing that many young people now face a more difficult employment situation than was once the case, it can be argued that on the whole it is still the older, male worker who is in the weakest position. The argument is based not so much on the share of the 60–65 age group in total unemployment, but on the exceptional vulnerability of older workers to unemployment and the length of time they are likely to be unemployed. In Daniel's words:

... if there is one rule it is that, among workers who lose their jobs, the older they are, the more difficulty they have in finding a new job, the longer their period out of work, and the more inferior any new job is likely to be to the one they lost. Equally, the older a worker is the less he is likely to retrain or move to find another job. The influence of age is overwhelming. It is far more important than jobs in the local labour market, or skill or qualifications.[13]

In short it is argued that while the burden of rising unemployment since 1974 has fallen heavily on both the young and the old, the *nature* of youth unemployment is quite different from the problem which affects older men.

Does the evidence support this conclusion? It is certainly true that age and duration of unemployment are positively associated (see Table 7).

Table 7

Unemployment by age and duration in Great Britain: Number and percentage of unemployed in each age group, January 1978

Men	Up to 20	20–40	40–55	55–65
One month–6 months	53·5	48·9	39·0	31·2
6 months–one year	19·2	17·3	17·1	18·7
Over one year	7·2	19·9	33·8	42·7

Source: *Department of Employment Gazette*, February 1978.

It is also true that the median duration of unemployment in the older age groups has increased, though at a slower rate than in the younger groups (see Table 8).

Table 8

Median male unemployment duration by age in Great Britain (weeks)

	Under 18	18–19	20–4	25–9	30–4	35–9	40–4	45–9	50–4	55–9	60–4
July 1966	1·9	2·7	3·0	4·1	5·1	6·6	8·0	9·4	14·2	21·3	32·0
July 1971	2·7	4·5	5·7	8·9	10·5	11·8	13·3	16·5	19·1	25·7	37·4
July 1973	2·3	3·1	5·0	9·2	12·7	17·6	21·6	27·5	32·9	44·8	50·7
July 1975	3·0	3·5	5·8	10·1	11·7	12·9	15·5	18·0	21·9	26·8	39·5
July 1977	4·3	8·5	13·1	18·0	20·1	22·6	24·7	29·1	34·1	37·7	46·3
January 1978	11·3	13·3	15·7	18·1	19·8	21·0	23·8	27·1	32·2	37·0	41·7

Source: *Department of Employment Gazette*, February 1973, June 1978.

However, the median age of the unemployed generally has been falling, and since 1975 long-term unemployment has also begun to affect more men in the prime working age groups. In January 1976 men in the 25–39 age group for the first time accounted for more than a fifth of those unemployed for more than one year, and by January 1978 this proportion had risen to 27 per cent. In short, unemployment is no longer associated so exclusively with the older age groups.

The position of the older worker in the labour market is, in fact, ambiguous. In Beveridge's words:

The influence of advancing years is not always unfavourable. There are some sorts of work at which men continue to become more skilful almost to the end of life itself. There are some industrial qualifications – proved trustworthiness, regularity, experience – to say nothing of old associations which get stronger not weaker with increasing age. There is, however, one industrial quality which almost inevitably deteriorates – adaptability – and this, in the flux of industry, is one of the most important qualities of all. The adverse influence of advancing years is thus seen less when it is a question of retaining old employment than when it is a question of finding new employers. The man of middle age who through trade depression or changes of method or the misfortunes of particular firms loses his ordinary place in industry is hard put to it to prove his worth among strangers. He may have admirable qualities, but he does not carry the proof of them with him as he does that of the years through which he has lived.[14]

To the extent that employers are becoming more reluctant to fill vacancies with unqualified young people, the position of the older, more experienced worker may well be strengthened.

The older age groups cannot, however, be regarded as in any sense homogeneous. Women over 55 are far less likely to be affected by unemployment than men, while skilled male workers are less likely to be affected than unskilled or white-collar workers. Motivation to work also varies considerably within the older groups. Daniel noted that, compared with those in the prime working age groups, both younger and older workers were less concerned about being out of work and attached less importance to finding a new job as quickly as possible:

As far as the younger men were concerned this was because they had often not yet taken on the responsibility of being heads of households and having dependents. The older men had passed the stages in the life cycle when the pressure from dependents was greatest and were often nearing official retirement age.[15]

One very important influence on motivation to work in the over-55 age group is, as might perhaps be expected, the available level of benefit. Thus Daniel found that over the age of 55, and particularly when they were nearing retirement age, 'those who had been made redundant or retired were much more likely to have received lump sum payments or pensions or both, and to have been less concerned about finding another job'.[16] The real difficulty arises in the case of those over 55 who are anxious to work. Surveys by the Department of Employment suggest that only a small minority of those over 55 have 'good, fair or reasonable' prospects of obtaining work and that, as with all other age groups, prospects decline with lengthening unemployment.[17] Older workers, therefore, tend to encounter greater handicaps in obtaining new jobs, however keen they may be to find work.

One might expect that as workers grow older, become less fit and find it more difficult to cope with their current job, the likelihood that they will be dismissed will increase. To some extent this expectation has been supported by Daniel's findings, though two points should be borne in mind. Firstly, since Daniel conducted his survey the Employment Protection Act has come into force and this legislation has probably strengthened the relative position of the older worker.[18] Secondly, Daniel found a very marked *occupational* difference in the treatment of workers over the age of 55. Managerial and white-collar employees were far more likely to be retired or made redundant on favourable terms than those in the manual grades.[19] In short, the age factor cannot be considered in isolation from the occupational characteristics of the unemployed.

Occupational unemployment

Unemployment does not affect every occupation to the same degree and, indeed, it would be very surprising if it did. Nevertheless, despite certain obvious limitations, the official statistics of occupational unemployment serve to highlight the more conspicuous mismatches in the labour market. The establishment of the Manpower Services Commission in 1974 signified the long-overdue acceptance in Britain of the concept of an 'active labour market policy'. In other words it has now been recognized that these mismatches cannot be removed simply by relying on the benign working of supply and demand. We shall offer a tentative evaluation of the labour market policy pursued in Britain since 1974 in Chapter Five. At this point we may simply observe that two mismatches are very much in evidence at the present time.

The first of these is the persistent over-supply of unskilled labour at every stage in the economic cycle. This mismatch may well be as old as industrial society itself. Beveridge, for example, observed: 'The glut of labour in the unskilled and unorganized occupations is notorious. Has there ever, in the big towns at least, been a time when employers could not get practically at a moment's notice all the labourers they required?'[20] Between 1959 and 1973 those described by the Department of Employment as 'general labourers' made up slightly more than half the total number of unemployed. A survey by the Department in June 1973 revealed that the age structure of this group was very similar to that of the unemployed as a whole, but that they had generally been out of work longer and their prospects of obtaining long-term work were thought to be relatively poor.[21] Between 1973 and 1976 the general labourers' share of total unemployment fell to about 40 per cent as other occupational groups were increasingly affected by the recession, but this was in no way indicative of a relative improvement in their market position. In June 1973 there were 14 unemployed labourers on the register for every notified vacancy in this category; by June 1975 the ratio had risen to 72. During the recession the labourers retained their disproportionate share of long-term unemployment. In June 1976, for example, they constituted 40 per cent of all unemployed men and 56 per cent of men unemployed for over a year. As marginal workers, the unskilled have always been the first to feel the effects of a recession and the last to benefit from a boom. Since there is a strong likelihood that the number of unskilled jobs in the economy will continue to decline, the underlying rate of unemployment in this group will almost certainly continue to rise.

By contrast, over the post-war period as a whole there has been a persistent shortage of skilled men. At the peak of the last boom in 1973 the number of notified vacancies for skilled men exceeded the number of unemployed in this category by about 50 per cent. The same was broadly true of women in the clerical and related grades, while skilled manual women enjoyed an even more favourable market position. With the onset of the recession in 1975 the excess demand for craftsmen as recorded by the ratio of registered unemployment to notified vacancies disappeared. Indeed, between June 1973 and June 1976 unemployment in the skilled manual workers' group rose faster (by 194 per cent) than in any other occupational group. Yet throughout the recession a minority of employers covered by the regular CBI surveys of business intentions, especially in engineering, reported that they were still short of skilled labour. The following table of comparative unemployment and vacancy figures (Table 9) helps to put this problem in perspective.

At first glance these figures seem remarkable in so far as they suggest that an overall increase in registered unemployment of about 75 per cent between March 1975 and March 1978 was accompanied by a *rise* in unfilled vacancies of slightly over 3 per cent. But their reliability as an index of labour market activity is severely qualified by the fact that by no means all vacancies are notified to employment offices, while the proportion notified varies between occupational groups. Nevertheless they tend to reinforce the conclusion that even during a severe recession skilled manual workers can expect to enjoy a much more favourable ratio of unemployed to vacancies than any other occupational group.

Within the craftsmen's group there seem to be marked variations in the demand for specific skills. In the engineering and

Table 9

Broad summary of the occupational analysis of numbers unemployed and notified vacancies unfilled in Great Britain, 1975–7

Occupational group	March 1975 Registered unemployed	Notified vacancies	March 1976 Registered unemployed	Notified vacancies	March 1977 Registered unemployed	Notified vacancies
Managerial & professional	48,810	22,095	87,968	14,225	104,286	16,781
Clerical & related	99,265	24,523	181,008	21,387	186,861	28,586
Other non-manual	29,795	13,966	68,958	11,950	76,712	15,506
Craft & similar occupations	93,382	43,934	161,972	39,427	160,983	48,246
General labourers	274,043	30,648	441,513	6,495	465,537	9,606
Other manual occupations	199,057	42,858	313,883	59,038	321,730	65,448
Total: all occupations	744,252	178,024	1,255,302	142,522	1,316,109	184,173

Source: *Department of Employment Gazette*, various issues.

related industries, for example, the number of notified vacancies in December 1977 for toolmakers and machine-tool-setter operators exceeded the number of registered unemployed in these two categories, whereas skilled welders faced an unemployment-vacancy ratio of more than eight to one.[22] Nevertheless, in nearly all skilled manual jobs in the engineering industry the unemployment-vacancy ratio was lower in December 1977 than it had been two years before, despite the broadly stagnant level of output in the industry during the intervening period. Even more significant was the fact that for about half the skilled engineering jobs, reported shortages in December 1977 were already greater than in December 1972, when output was expanding rapidly and total unemployment was about 50 per cent lower.[23] One graphic and much-publicized illustration of the growing significance of skill shortages was provided in June 1978 when ICI announced that they had decided to close down part of their chemical plant at Wilton (situated in an area of above-average unemployment) because they could not recruit 170 much-needed instrument artificers. The reasons why the supply of skilled labour has not improved during the recent recession, and may actually have deteriorated even further, will be discussed in Chapter Five. All we need to note here is that a solution to the problem will involve far more than simply expanding the Manpower Services Commission's current training programme.

Two other features of the present pattern of occupational unemployment should be noted. Although much publicity has been given in recent years to the problem of executive redundancy, the official statistics suggest that between 1973 and 1978 male unemployment in the managerial and professional grades increased only slightly faster than the trend in total male unemployment.[24] Employment prospects for those in this group remain as good as they are in the skilled manual grades.[25] By contrast those in the clerical and related grades have relatively poor prospects, largely because about half the people in this group are aged 60 or over. But taken as a whole, unemployment in the clerical group increased at only half the overall rate between 1973 and 1978. It would be reasonable to conclude, therefore, that while all occupational groups have felt the effects of the recent recession, the brunt of rising unemployment has been borne, as in previous recessions, by the unskilled.

The geography of unemployment

Ever since the 1920s certain regions have consistently experienced higher-than-average rates of unemployment, but although regional disparities are still in evidence, they are by no means as sharp as they were during the inter-war period. In 1936, for example, unemployment in Scotland, the North East and the North West was about three times the rate in London and the South East, while in Wales it was nearly five times the London rate. In the post-war period these inter-regional differences were diminished by a gradual diversification in the economies of the relatively depressed regions.[26] Since 1973 all regions have been affected by rising unemployment and in general the regional rates have moved in unison (see Figure 2).

It is generally believed that in regions of relatively high unemployment, the average *duration* of unemployment tends to be longer and the proportion of young people out of work is somewhat higher than in the low unemployment regions. Yet an

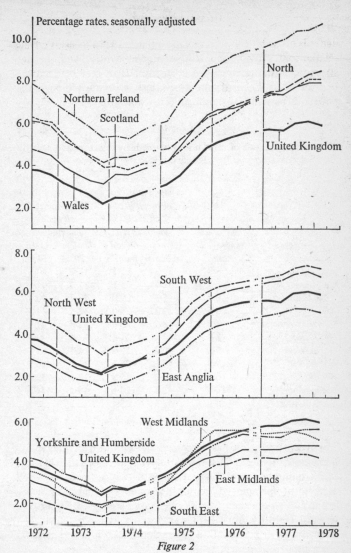

Figure 2

Regional unemployment rates, United Kingdom

Source: *Economic Trends,* May 1978.

analysis of the official statistics for January 1978 suggests that the relationship between the level of unemployment and the age structure of the unemployed is stronger than that between the level of unemployment and its average duration, although the pattern is by no means uniform (see Table 10).

Table 10

Regional analysis of male unemployment by duration and age; January 1978

Region	Male unemployment rate %	Long-term male unemployed as proportion of all male unemployed		Proportion of all male unemployed	
		Over 6 months	Over 12 months	Under 20	Over 40
South East	5·8	39·2	21·1	11·2	40·3
East Midlands	6·3	41·6	25·1	11·6	44·1
West Midlands	6·5	47·3	29·0	13·4	40·3
East Anglia	6·6	39·2	24·0	11·5	44·7
Yorks/Humberside	7·3	42·2	25·7	12·4	41·2
South West	8·9	42·2	24·8	13·4	40·3
North West	9·2	49·2	29·9	14·7	35·6
Wales	9·9	44·2	26·6	13·6	36·3
North	10·4	46·0	28·5	13·3	39·2
Scotland	10·6	42·1	24·6	17·5	34·6
Great Britain	8·1	43·3	25·4	13·2	39·3

Source: *Department of Employment Gazette*, February 1978.

The recent recession has increased the duration of unemployment more rapidly in the low unemployment regions than in those at the opposite end of the scale. In April 1975, for example, 52 per cent of unemployed men in the South East had been on the register for more than two months, compared with 64 per cent in the North. By April 1978, the proportion in the North had increased to 77 per cent, but in the South East it had risen to 71 per cent.

Surveys by the Department of Employment have not revealed any other striking differences between the regional characteristics of the unemployed. In June 1973 and again in June 1976 employment offices in all regions considered that between 19 and 29 per cent of their unemployed men had 'good or fair' prospects of obtaining work. The regions with high average unemployment rates on the whole had slightly higher proportions with 'good or fair' prospects than the regions of lower unemployment. This mainly reflects the different age structure of unemployment in the regions, and the fact that younger men are considered to have much better prospects of obtaining work than older men. In July 1976, for example, the percentage of men aged 55 and over (out of the total aged 18 and over) ranged from 17 per cent in the North West to 28 per cent in the South West. It must be remembered, however, that in all regions there is considerable movement on and off the register, especially among the younger age groups, and, even in high unemployment areas, many unemployed people find jobs every month.[27]

The reasons why certain regions are prone to relatively high rates of unemployment may be found in their economic structure. The depressed regions are commonly regarded as depressed either because they are heavily dependent on declining industries or because they are geographically remote from the main centres of economic activity. An undue reliance on one or more declining industries also has a negative spin-off on the growth of alternative industries and services in the region because it reduces the rate of growth of incomes per head.[28] The Northern region, for example, lost about 170,000 jobs in its old industries (mainly coal, shipbuilding and steel) between 1959 and 1974, for a gain of only 129,000 jobs in other industries and services.[29] In Scotland over the period 1965–75, the primary and manufacturing sectors together shed 157,000 jobs, while the service sector created only 118,000 jobs. The same pattern has been repeated at local level in other regions. Bradford, for example, was heavily dependent on the wool textile industry which as recently as 1959 provided work for about one-third of the city's employed population. Between 1959 and 1974, however, employment in wool textiles fell by 50 per cent and although the service sector expanded, it did so at a slower rate. A further problem posed by the growth of service employment is that it has tended to create more jobs for women than for men. Thus in Bradford between 1971 and 1976 women lost 7,300 jobs in the manufacturing sector as a whole but gained 9,600 in the service industries. By contrast, men lost 6,600 jobs in manufacturing for a gain of only 3,100 in the service industries. One symptom of this structural weakness is that in most years since 1967 Bradford's unemployment rate has been higher than both the national and the regional average.[30]

The experience of Bradford – and indeed that of many other cities in recent years – serves to remind us that structural imbalances can develop at local as much as at regional level. Indeed a regional unemployment problem may simply be the summation of several local problems, none of which need be precisely the same. It is generally known, for example, that within every region there are certain blackspots which return relatively high rates of unemployment at every stage of the economic cycle, and there are other localities which consistently do far better than the regional average. The same pattern of local variations can usually be found within a particular city or conurbation. Liverpool, for example, has consistently returned the highest rate of local unemployment in the North West at the peaks and troughs of successive economic cycles. Yet within Liverpool itself during the recent recession the level of unemployment in the central 'core' area was nearly three times the average for the city as a whole.[31]

The highest unemployment rates in the country are now to be found in some of the inner residential areas of our largest towns and cities. The reasons why this has happened are all too familiar. While most inner-city areas have lost population over the past decade, jobs have disappeared at a faster rate as manufacturing industry has moved out to the suburbs. As Pahl has noted:

Those growth industries which are expanding the most rapidly tend to be those which have a high demand for skills, a high ratio of managers to managed and a favourable ratio of floor-space to worker. Space and skilled workers are the crucial locational factors and the peripheries of city regions appear to be ideal sites ... The effect of this peripheral expansion may be to limit the opportunities for social mobility by those in the central cities, hemmed in by middle-class suburbs and offered employment either in old-established and possibly declining manufacturing industries, where the wages are often low (e.g. the textile industry), or the service sector, where opportunities for training and advancement may be less good.[32]

Liverpool provides us with one of the most glaring examples of the process described by Pahl. Government aid to Merseyside has helped to bring in 100,000 new jobs since the early 1960s but these are concentrated around the periphery of the conurbation, while Liverpool itself has lost a greater number of jobs. The inner areas of Liverpool traditionally depended on the docks and their ancillary industries and transport services, all of which have declined rapidly in recent years. Once an inner area begins to decline, the all-too-familiar problems of social deprivation and environmental blight emerge which help to discourage the influx of new sources of employment and induce those people with relatively good prospects to move out. In this way an inner area can quickly go into a self-reinforcing, downward spiral.

The social and demographic structure of many inner-city areas is, therefore, particularly favourable to high levels of unemployment. As the younger, more skilled elements in the population move out, so they leave behind a pool of ageing, unskilled labour which has been discarded by the declining industries and has generally poor prospects of finding new work. In the words of one observer:

A significant minority of these residents are poorly educated, are unskilled, have incomes too low to travel far, and perceptions too limited to know the possibilities. They could perform the heavy, simple jobs needing much strength but little skill, that were once plentiful. But in the new age of the automated machine and the computer, there is no place for their modest talents.[33]

In the inner areas of Bradford, for example, over 60 per cent of unemployed men in 1976 were unskilled (compared with the national average for this group of 40 per cent) and about half of them had been out of work for over a year. In inner Liverpool in 1976 over 60 per cent of the unskilled unemployed had been out of work for more than half of the preceding five years. In central London the problem of mismatch has been greatly aggravated by the massive development of tertiary industries, all of which provide numerous white-collar jobs requiring, even at the lowest levels, certain basic skills. But, in Hall's words:

Many among the inner-city work-force simply lack these skills. The older ones will presumably never have them. Too many of the younger ones are not acquiring them either, yet have totally unrealistic job expectations. So the paradox emerges, notorious to any employer – or consumer – in London: high unemployment a couple of miles from the centre, coupled with chronic shortages of reliable labour for basic jobs like typing or van-driving or answering the phone.[34]

An additional and increasingly important problem in many inner areas is the high and rising unemployment rate among the non-white population, especially in the under-25 age group. In Bradford, for example, in July 1977 nearly 50 per cent of the non-white school-leavers immediately became unemployed, compared with 17 per cent of all school-leavers.[35] There are two possible reasons for heavy unemployment among the non-white population. They are heavily concentrated in the inner city, where employment opportunities are least plentiful, and they are essentially a marginal source of labour.[36] They take worse-quality work at each level of skill and are probably the first to feel the effects of either a 'shut-out' or a 'shake-out' of labour.[37] If, therefore, a hard core of 'unemployables' does exist, it is likely to be found in the inner-city areas and to be composed largely of old, unskilled whites and young, unskilled blacks.

We may conclude this section by simply observing that the old habit of defining Britain's unemployment problem in regional terms seems increasingly inappropriate. Regional disparities still exist but they are by no means as glaring as they used to be. A potentially more rewarding form of analysis lies in comparing different local rates and investigating why these rates differ. It will be found that within a given region there are likely to be some local economies which have serious structural problems and thus an equally serious unemployment problem. The inner areas of many large industrial towns and cities provide the most glaring examples of localized structural imbalance. The question of whether these structural problems should be tackled by broad, national policies operating at national level will be discussed in Chapter Five.

Summary

The suggestion that unemployment in Britain has in recent years acquired certain recognizably American characteristics finds some support in the experience of the non-white population and those who live in the inner-city areas. Beyond that, the predominant impression is one of continuity with the past. Unemployment does not fall like 'God's gentle rain' on all groups and individuals and never has done. Pollard's description of the differential impact of mass unemployment in the early 1930s bears a striking resemblance to the problem as it exists at the present time:

There were boys and girls, shunted into dead-end jobs when leaving school and then thrown on the labour market when old enough to claim full wages, without skill and without a trade, and there were the youths who never secured a steady job at all, even for a time. There were the older men who found it impossible, once they were dismissed, ever to gain new employment, and whose only hope lay in by-employment, such as allotment-keeping or poultry farming. There were labourers with large families who secured almost as much, if not more, on the dole because of the family allowance element in it, as when they were working, and who had therefore no incentive to seek work ...[38]

Other groups, by contrast, are far less vulnerable to unemployment. Indeed, the traditional shortfall in the supply of certain kinds of skilled labour seems if anything to have become more pronounced during the recent recession.

The persistence of certain shortages of labour at a time when total unemployment has reached a post-war record underlines the failure of market forces to correct the most conspicuous mismatches. But then, of course, it would be a mistake to regard the labour market as a homogeneous entity. The persistence of differential rates of unemployment both between and within the regions suggests that labour mobility in Britain is low and that for most workers the labour market is essentially local.[39] Some areas have well-balanced economies, others have serious structural problems. Such problems are generally most acute in the inner city, where the outward movement of industry has typically left behind a labour force heavily slanted towards marginal groups who are prone to relatively high rates of unemployment at all stages in the economic cycle. It would be naive to assume that these structural problems can be solved simply by raising aggregate demand to an 'appropriate' level, or by introducing import controls, or by some other form of macro-economic wizardry. Indeed, there are no quick and painless solutions to any of the mismatches outlined in this chapter.

The over-supply of unqualified young people is undoubtedly the most serious mismatch confronting policy-makers at the present time. To some extent, of course, the recent shut-out of school-leavers simply reflects the low level of aggregate demand. But the erosion of job opportunities for the least skilled members of this age-group may also reflect a longer-term change in the demand for labour, the effects of which are cumulative and may not therefore become fully apparent for several years. At the present time there is little doubt that those who leave school without any qualifications, who live in areas of relatively high unemployment and who are psychologically ill-prepared for their entry into work, are more and more likely to face repeated and perhaps prolonged spells of unemployment. In short, the mere fact of their youth may no longer compensate for their lack of skill or aptitude. The problem facing younger *men* is likely to become even more acute if the long-term fall in male employment continues. Unlike those in the over-55 age group, the young unemployed still have their working lives in front of them and a bad start may in some cases have serious long-term consequences. Successive surveys by the Department of Employment suggest that for *all* age groups both keenness to work and the prospects of obtaining work decline as the duration of unemployment increases. We must therefore face the possibility that many of those young people who have spent a large proportion of their time on the unemployment register may eventually form a hard core of people who, even at the peak of a cycle, are virtually unemployable.

Some readers may, however, object to this prediction on the grounds that it simply assumes the continuation of present trends. If full employment as we knew it up to a few years ago can be restored, then, they might argue, the problem of long-term unemployment among young people, if not among older workers, should largely disappear. Even if full employment means running the economy at a higher level of unemployment than was customary in the post-war period, surely it is not beyond the wit of governments to devise a labour market strategy which will prevent the emergence of young 'unemployables'? It is to these two important questions that we must now turn.

CHAPTER FOUR

Is Full Employment Possible?

> Suppose that at 4 per cent unemployment the bargaining
> power of the trade unions were so great that the general
> level of money wage rates rose by 5 per cent per annum,
> and that it required an unemployment percentage of
> 10 per cent so to reduce the bargaining position of the
> trade unions that the general level of money wage rates
> was not pushed up by more than the tolerable 2 per cent
> per annum. Society would be faced with a most bitter
> dilemma.
>
> Professor J. E. Meade, 1948

Is it realistic for policy-makers to think in terms of restoring
employment to the levels which were customary in Britain and
elsewhere up to the 1970s? Many economists now believe that the
historical trade-off relationship between unemployment and
inflation has deteriorated in recent years to a point where it is no
longer practicable to think in terms of restoring full employment
through conventional demand management. In the words of a
recent OECD report: '... the biggest single constraint in achieving reasonable rates of growth in the future – and the greatest
barrier to a rapid return to full employment – is the increased
tendency towards inflation, both domestically and internationally,
which has emerged over the last few years'.[1] The belief that
inflation is the 'father and mother' of unemployment has
strongly influenced the policies pursued by all Western governments since 1974–5 and largely explains why politicians and
economists alike are now very reticent about the prospects for
restoring 'full' employment. By contrast, some people reject the
proposition that there is even a long-term trade-off between
unemployment and inflation. In Field's words: 'Since 1974 we
have seen a massive press-ganging of workers into Britain's
conscript army of the unemployed to fight the war against

inflation. Yet ... there is no evidence to support the view that increasing the numbers of unemployed decreases the inflationary pressures in the British economy.'[2] They argue, therefore, that full employment can be restored by expanding aggregate demand and protecting the balance of payments by means of import controls (see Chapter Five).

It must be remembered, however, that when economists speak of 'full employment' they are in fact referring to the full employment level of *unemployment*. It has always been recognized that even at the peak of a boom when industry is working flat out there will always be *some* people out of work. In his early study Beveridge described this phenomenon as the 'irreducible minimum' of unemployment.[3] The implication is that there will always be a certain proportion of workers who are either frictionally or structurally unemployed or virtually unemployable. Subsequently Beveridge defined full employment as a situation in which there would always be 'more vacant jobs than unemployed men' and suggested a figure of 3 per cent as a 'conservative' target for unemployment.[4] In the immediate post-war period most economists – including Keynes himself – thought in terms of a much higher average figure.[5] It was only the experience of the years between 1948 and 1966, when unemployment was generally below 2 per cent, which encouraged economists and politicians alike to believe that full employment should normally be as full as this. Since then, of course, the full employment level of unemployment in Britain and in most other Western countries appears to have risen, although there is little agreement on the question of where this level now stands or on whether a further rise is inevitable in the foreseeable future. Before we can answer the question posed above, therefore, we must briefly consider the alternative concepts of full employment with which policy-makers are confronted.

The Phillips Curve

Probably the best-known definition of full employment derives from the conventional belief that inflation and unemployment are inversely correlated. In Britain this belief has proved extremely influential with economic strategists since the late 1940s. As Godley and Shepherd observed in 1964:

One of the main aims of short-term economic policy in Britain has been to regulate the pressure of demand for labour, and to keep the fluctuations of the unemployment percentage within fairly narrow limits. High unemployment is obviously undesirable; at the other end of the scale, if the pressure of demand for labour is too strong, this tends to lead to excessively high wage increases and to balance of payment difficulties. It is for the government to decide at what pressure it wishes to run the economy, and to try to keep it there.[6]

In short, the full employment level of unemployment was a matter for policy-makers themselves to decide in accordance with other economic and indeed political criteria. One way of measuring this level is to compare the various rates of unemployment at which successive governments have taken reflationary action.[7] Up to 1966 a level of 2 per cent unemployment was enough to provoke an expansion of demand; by 1971, however, this had risen to 3·6 per cent and in 1977–8 a rate of nearly 6 per cent was sufficient to justify only a very modest reflationary package.

This definition of full employment is based on the Phillips Curve. Phillips examined the relationship between changes in money wage rates and the level of unemployment over the period 1861 to 1957 and found that low unemployment was associated with large increases in money wages and vice versa.[8] *A priori*, one would expect to find a strong relationship between inflation and unemployment in an unorganized labour market in which the interplay of supply and demand was not inhibited by institutional controls. Not surprisingly Phillips obtained the best results from the data covering the period up to 1913, but in the post-war environment the Curve seems fundamentally implausible. Firstly, it relies on the questionable assumption that the official unemployment rate accurately reflects the underlying pressure of aggregate demand in the economy. Secondly, it suggests that falling demand for labour in general will reduce the bargaining power of the trade unions. There is no evidence, however, to suggest that labour markets work in this extremely simple way. Even in the severest recessions the demand for *all* types of labour does not fall and, as we saw in the previous chapter, unemployment invariably affects some groups far more than others. Nor is there any evidence to suggest that trade union behaviour is significantly affected by the level of unemployment *per se*. In Blackaby's words:

Those trade unions which, in any round of wage negotiations, tend to set the target figure which subsequent negotiators aim to reach are not usually in industries which feel themselves under much threat from unemployment; or if they do feel such a threat, they may well not be persuaded that a rapid increase in money earnings would increase unemployment. Unemployment tends to fall not on those leading the wage bargaining process but on those who are on the margin of the labour force.[9]

In any case, during the late 1960s the simple relationship depicted in the Phillips Curve broke down in both Britain and other Western countries as rising unemployment and accelerating inflation occurred simultaneously. There is no consensus among economists on the reasons for this breakdown, and it is likely that there were several contributory factors. There was a general tendency for real disposable incomes to rise more slowly than productivity in the period 1966–8, so that the 'wage explosions' which began in 1968 may be seen as an attempt by organized labour to recover the lost ground. But did this increasing militancy reflect a permanent shift in the bargaining aspirations of the trade unions, or was it a delayed adjustment to the inflationary climate created by years of full employment? Economists of the 'monetarist' school have argued that the operation of all Western economies at very high levels of employment for a prolonged period had by the late 1960s generated a rise in inflationary *expectations* which was simply reinforced by the wage explosions of 1968–70.[10] By 1972, therefore, the supposed trade-off between inflation and unemployment had begun to deteriorate. But the massive rise in oil and other import prices which began in 1972 and lasted until 1974 generated very strong inflationary expectations which in turn produced a more rapid deterioration. This was particularly true in Britain where, for electoral reasons, the Labour government elected in 1974 failed to restrain aggregate demand until the rate of inflation had reached record levels. The more deeply embedded that expectations of rapid inflation become, the less effect a rise in unemployment will have on the actual rate of inflation. If the 'expectations' hypothesis is valid, however, it suggests that the apparent collapse of the Phillips Curve *need* not be permanent. If the money supply is rigorously controlled and inflationary expectations are gradually brought down, it should in fact be possible to *improve* the trade-off between inflation and unemployment. It has also been argued, however, that after the experience of recent years expectations will not be changed so easily and to that extent the deterioration in the unemployment-inflation relationship may prove to be irreversible.

An alternative approach to defining full employment has been offered by Friedman. In brief, he suggests that there is a *natural* rate of unemployment in any economy which is synonymous with the full employment rate. This rate will be achieved when the supply of and demand for labour are in balance, which will only happen when the *real* wage rate (i.e. the real cost of employing labour) is at a level which will induce employers to expand recruitment. As Trevithick has pointed out, this definition is not essentially different from that advanced by pre-Keynesian economists.[11] It relies on changes in the real wage rate to achieve full employment, at which point the natural rate of unemployment will be the same as the actual rate and there will be neither upward nor downward pressure on the rate of inflation. If an economy is operating at a level of unemployment above the natural rate, then the government can increase demand and reduce unemployment. It cannot, however, push the actual rate *below* the natural rate without generating more inflation. In Friedman's words: 'The only way unemployment can be kept below the natural rate is by an *ever-accelerating* inflation which always keeps current inflation ahead of anticipated inflation.'[12] His explanation of Britain's rising rate of inflation since the mid-1960s depends therefore on the proposition that successive governments have sought to keep unemployment below the natural rate. Thus, while there is a short-term trade-off between inflation and unemployment, in the long run it is only the natural rate of unemployment which is consistent with a stable rate of inflation.

But what determines the natural rate of unemployment and how can we measure it? In Laidler's words:

It would be determined by the way in which the geographical distribution of job vacancies was matched up with the geographical distribution of the unemployed; by the way in which the skill mix required to fill vacancies was matched by that among the unemployed: that is, by the rapidity of adjustment of supply to demand in the labour market. The age distribution of the labour force would influence it, as should the educational characteristics of the labour force ... It would not be a variable which could be expected to remain constant. It would be a 'natural' unemployment rate in the sense that its value was determined by the structure of the 'real' side of the economy – the institutions of the labour market, etc. – and not in the sense that it was unvarying.[13]

The natural rate thus represents the amount of structural and frictional unemployment which is left in the economy when supply and demand are in balance. It can be lowered by policies designed to improve the working of the labour market but *not* by conventional attempts to increase the general level of economic activity. Presumably the natural rate might be expected to increase if for some reason structural weaknesses in the economy were getting worse. But how do we know whether it is rising or falling unless we can measure it? Laidler concedes that the natural rate would be 'extremely hard to assess' but suggests that it may be near 2 per cent. Such a low figure would, if it were valid, obviously pull the rug beneath Friedman's argument that unemployment in Britain had been repeatedly pushed *below* its natural rate. More recent estimates indicate that it is more likely to be about 3·75 per cent, a figure which seems more realistic but may still be on the low side. Since it is virtually impossible to draw a clear distinction for purposes of measurement between demand-deficient and non-demand-deficient unemployment, it would be unwise to invest *any* estimate of the natural rate with too much significance.

The Keynesian definition of full employment is akin to Friedman's natural-rate hypothesis in so far as it presupposes that real wages will be at their market-clearing level. When the labour market is in equilibrium, *involuntary* unemployment will be zero and employment will be full. If substantial involuntary unemployment exists then real wages must be too high. But, Keynes argued, it is impossible to cut real wages by getting workers to accept a general reduction in their money wages. The main stumbling-block lies in the rigid structure of wage *differentials*. Work groups and their organizations will resist cuts in their money wages because of the effects on the structure of relativities and differentials. Most wage bargains are ultimately bargains over wage differentials. Differentials have a market function in so far as they can influence the supply of labour in a particular industry or occupation. But they also have a social function in the sense that they 'indicate society's assessment of the value of a particular job and are frequently interpreted by individuals in specific occupations as indicators of status and a general sort of esteem'.[14] The only way in which real wages can be reduced, therefore, is by allowing the price level to rise faster than money wage rates. There is no reason to suppose that high unemployment will depress the rate of growth of money wages.[15] Consequently it is quite possible for a large amount of involuntary unemployment to exist alongside a fully anticipated rate of inflation. A restrictive demand policy may simply increase unemployment and leave the rate of wage inflation unchecked. It follows that an incomes policy may well be necessary if inflation expectations are to be reduced.

The Keynesian yardstick in its simplest form suggests that since most of the recent growth in unemployment cannot be attributed to an increase in voluntary unemployment, the British economy has not been at full employment since the mid-1960s. But the situation has deteriorated since the early 1970s because real wages have been too high. The explosive increase in oil and other import prices between 1972 and 1974 implied a major shift in the terms of trade against all Western countries. The British economy was in a particularly vulnerable position because its average import propensity had been rising sharply since 1966. But the effects of this shift on real incomes in Britain were delayed firstly by the index-linked incomes policy of 1974 and secondly by the collapse of the 'social contract' in 1974–5. In the absence of a strong incomes policy money wages were allowed to rise slightly faster than prices generally. All the adjustment had therefore to be taken on profits and the balance of payments, with disastrous consequences for both. It has been estimated that by mid-1975, when the Labour government was finally forced to grasp the incomes policy nettle, average real wages were at least 6 per cent higher than they should have been.[16] Consequently the inevitable adjustment came through *total* real incomes and manifested itself in an explosive rise in unemployment. If productivity growth had continued at its trend rate of about 3 per cent during the recession, unemployment would have risen even more. In fact, however, output fell much more sharply than employment, leading to a decline in productivity during 1975. The subsequent recovery was extremely slow and even in 1977 productivity was still lower than it had been in 1973. This implies that in 1975 the excess real wage was more than twice as high as the 6 per cent quoted above, and that despite the fall in real earnings between 1975 and 1977 the average real wage was still about 6 per cent too high in the latter year.

This would explain why unemployment remained extremely sluggish on its high plateau during 1977–8. The government could in theory have made a real impact on unemployment if it had adopted a much lower norm for settlements for the pay round of 1977–8 than the 10 per cent which was allowed and had thus engineered a further decline in average real earnings. Alternatively it could have reduced the real supply cost of labour by cutting employers' national insurance contributions. In practice, of course, it did the opposite. During 1977–8 money earnings rose by about 15 per cent, or roughly twice as fast as price inflation, income tax was reduced and employers' national insurance contributions were increased. The previous fall in real wages was thus reversed and the supply cost of labour rose. The conclusion must be that since real wages were moving in the wrong direction during 1978, unemployment will begin to rise again in 1978–9.

In summary, therefore, it may be said that none of the definitions of full employment discussed above provides much comfort for policy-makers in the circumstances of the late 1970s. The Phillips Curve which once offered policy-makers the freedom to choose their own level of full employment has either broken down completely or shifted so far outwards as to remove the element of discretion for all practical purposes. Indeed, it may be that the Curve merely depicts a relationship which is not causal at all but merely coincidental. The 'natural rate' hypothesis denies that policy-makers have such discretion anyway but it in turn gives them little practical assistance. The analysis presented in Chapter Three suggests that in Britain the natural rate may well have increased in recent years in so far as structural unemployment has risen, but until the rate itself can be quantified (which, given the limitations of the available data, is impossible), we have no way of knowing how far the actual unemployment rate is above the natural rate. The Keynesian approach does not suffer from the same imprecision in the sense that it is possible to calculate how far real wages would have to fall before they reached their market-clearing level.[17] But Keynesians must also assume that even if the government pursued the correct policies, the trade unions would be prepared to see the real wages of their members fall until full employment was restored. The experience of 1975-8 suggests that such an assumption is unrealistic, particularly if real wages are a long way above their equilibrium level at the outset.

Are we to conclude from this evidence, as indeed so many pre-Keynesian economists did, that it is only the short-sighted resistance of the trade unions to reductions in real wages which is preventing the restoration of full employment? This brings us to the familiar proposition that the monopoly power of the trade unions has increased over the post-war period as a whole to such an extent that they now determine the rate of inflation and thus the level of unemployment. Keynes, of course, denied that the trade unions were responsible for the level of unemployment between the wars. But contemporary Keynesians could argue that the unions, especially those in Britain, have become bigger, stronger and more militant since Keynes's day. One need only compare the results of the coal-miners' strike in 1926 with those of the similar stoppages of 1972 and 1974 to appreciate how the balance of power in industry has changed. Why, then, are they using their power in such a destructive way? One possible answer is, quite simply, that Britain's trade union leaders are 'astonishingly stupid' by comparison with their counterparts elsewhere. In Lord Kahn's words:

> Their sole concern is with the level of the real wage in the immediate future, as opposed to the rate of increase in the real wage. By insisting on unduly high wage increases, they force the government and the central bank to adopt restrictive measures and they undermine the confidence of employers. One important link in the chain of causation is our chronically adverse balance of payments, caused by our failure to be competitive. The result is not only unemployment and surplus physical capacity, but a low rate of productive investment, resulting in a low rate of growth of productivity and a low rate of increase in the real wage.[18]

The question of what lies behind such apparently irrational behaviour is not satisfactorily answered by simple generalizations about relative stupidity. There are in fact two possible explanations, neither of which necessarily excludes the other. One is that trade union bargaining objectives are strongly influenced by the fragmented institutional framework within which collective bargaining is conducted. In Blackaby's words:

> There is, in wage bargaining, a clear conflict between what would be rational behaviour for all negotiators if they negotiated together at one time, and what is rational behaviour for the individual negotiating group. Trade union leaders are well aware that large increases in aggregate money earnings are pointless, and indeed are likely to be counter-productive ... The individual negotiator, on the other hand, has a different set of considerations in mind. He is not concerned with the macro-economic consequences of any award which he negotiates, nor does he ask himself what will happen if all other negotiators obtain the same figure. For many negotiators, the prime consideration is to ensure that the group he represents does not fall behind: that it should at least get the 'going figure' and if possible improve on it a little.[19]

There is no evidence to suggest that negotiators are doing anything more than articulate the aspirations of the workers they represent. Daniel, for example, has found the same dichotomy between macro- and micro-perspectives among the population as a whole:

Wage and salary earners respond in relation to their own pay according to their particular family circumstances and workplace relations, and the facts of life from their perspective, rather than the facts of life as they appear from a perspective derived from the management of the economy. For these reasons, concern about the general problem of inflation is relatively remote and abstract. Concern about personal earnings in relation to commitments and the rising cost of living is immediate and specific.[20]

Whether this dichotomy will be resolved by radical changes in the institutional framework of collective bargaining so that, for example, all major wage agreements are negotiated simultaneously, remains to be seen.

The second explanation of trade union behaviour is that union leaders largely react to pressures and events which they do not and cannot control. *Why* have the unions become more militant in recent years? The 'stupidity' of British trade union leaders is hardly a convincing explanation when it is remembered that the growth of militancy has been a general European phenomenon. The real reason may well lie in the general increase in inflation throughout the Western world associated with the increase in the world supply of money arising from the huge American balance of payments deficit which developed during the 1960s and has persisted ever since.[21] As a result the cost of living has accelerated, and trade unions have responded by negotiating wage agreements which seek both to compensate their members for past increases in inflation and to protect their living standards against the inflation which is anticipated in the period before the next agreement. Another source of pressure on workers' living standards has been the growing burden of direct taxation which rising government expenditure has generated.[22] Rising inflation and increasing tax 'bite' have combined to slow down the rate of growth in real incomes, hence the pressure for compensatory increases in money wages and salaries.

While the international dimensions of trade union militancy cannot be ignored, it must also be recognized that the problem of re-adjusting real wages to their full employment level will be particularly difficult in Britain. The fragmented institutional framework of wage determination makes it harder for trade unions, employers and politicians to achieve a workable agreement on macro-economic objectives, even assuming they have the political will to do so; the possibility of reforming collective bargaining will be discussed in Chapter Five. Also, the extent to which real wages must be reduced is strongly influenced by the growth of productivity, and in Britain the level of productivity is comparatively low. This problem is closely associated with that of excess real wages and thus of unemployment, which we will now discuss.

A productivity constraint?

Until the onset of the recent recession, the productivity performance of British industry was undoubtedly improving. Output per person employed in manufacturing increased from an average growth rate of 2·4 per cent in the period 1955–60 to 4·3 per cent in the period 1969–73. The problem is that not only has Britain's productivity performance fallen short of that achieved by its major industrial competitors, but that the marked improvement since 1967 seems to have been achieved at the expense of employment. Jones's estimates, for example, suggest that in 1955 labour productivity in Britain was significantly higher than in France, West Germany and Italy, yet by 1974 France and West Germany had gained a 30 per cent advantage.[23] In manufacturing industry, comparisons of productivity levels are even more unfavourable to Britain (see Table 11).

Table 11

Levels of output per person employed in sub-sectors of manufacturing, 1970 (UK = 100)

	Food, drink, tobacco	Textiles, leather, clothing	Chemicals	Basic metals	Metal products	Other manufacturing
Belgium	163	129	160	271	156	131
France	197	109	164	268	177	141
W. Germany	153	120	147	258	153	175
Italy	120	82	133	215	138	95
Netherlands	184	141	188	272	178	156

Source: *National Institute Economic Review.*

What accounts for the low average level of labour productivity in British industry? One factor may be the apparent reluctance of some firms to invest in up-to-date, labour-saving equipment. The Ryder report on British Leyland, for example, argued that the firm's most serious weakness was that a large proportion of its plant and equipment was 'old, out-dated and inefficient'. A low average level of fixed assets per man was held to be the main reason for the company's inadequate output. It has also been argued, however, that low investment is essentially a symptom of low *total* productivity. If the rate of return on a given amount of capital and labour is unattractive to investors, then new investment will be discouraged. In Britain over the period 1964–76 a shareholder paying tax at the standard rate would have received a (net of tax) rate of return on his equity investment of *minus* 2·7 per cent per annum.[24] In these circumstances, it is hardly surprising that funds which might have gone into industrial equities have instead been diverted into more profitable channels. Inadequate investment has undoubtedly helped to perpetuate the productivity gap between Britain and its major competitors, but it is by no means the sole cause of this gap.

There is a large and growing body of evidence to suggest that behavioural and institutional factors have played a key role in Britain's productivity performance. A report by the Central Policy Review Staff on the motorcar industry (1975), for example, concluded that 'with the same power at his elbow and doing the same job, a continental car-assembly worker normally produces twice as much as his British counterpart'. The report attributed this alarming productivity differential to a combination of technical and behavioural factors, notably overmanning, slow pace of work, quality faults, high fixed overheads and strikes. Broadly the same picture emerges from a survey of manufacturing industry in the West Midlands. The authors of this survey found that an unduly high proportion of working hours were spent unproductively and concluded that production levels could in many cases be doubled without any new investment.[25] Other studies have indicated that although the inefficient use of manpower is not the only cause of low productivity, it is often very important. Managerial weaknesses have frequently been identified as a principal reason for the misuse of manpower, but the behaviour of workgroups and their organizations must also be emphasized. Employers tend to argue that they would be more willing to introduce labour-saving technology if the trade unions adopted a more flexible approach to manning standards and demarcation. This argument must be treated with some reserve as a *general* explanation of low productivity in view of the fact that some companies have managed to negotiate improvements in efficiency with union representatives, but it does introduce an issue which is directly relevant to this discussion, namely the relationship between productivity and employment security.

Common sense suggests that employees who feel insecure in their jobs will tend to cling on to those working practices which preserve traditional manning standards. But, as Pratten has pointed out, 'in practice it is often difficult to determine whether insecurity of employment has led to reluctance to accept change, or whether reluctance to accept change has led to inefficient use of manpower, and hence job insecurity'.[26] It is certainly worth noting that in the period 1948–66, when unemployment was generally low and in certain regions the demand for labour exceeded the supply, productivity growth was very sluggish. During the 1950s some economists argued that a persistent shortage of labour would encourage firms to use their manpower resources more effectively and invest in labour-saving techniques. Another school of thought maintained that a persistently high level of demand removed the incentive to improve efficiency, encouraged employers to hoard scarce labour and facilitated the survival of inefficient firms. The pessimists were probably right. The relative insensitivity of the labour market to fluctuations in aggregate demand suggests that during recessions employers tended to hoard labour in anticipation of the next upswing. In this sense it could be said that up to the mid-1960s, full employment was achieved only at the price of widespread *under*-employment and inefficiency. After the severe deflation of July 1966, however, employers dis-hoarded labour on an unprecedented scale and the underlying growth rate of productivity increased quite sharply.[27] It could be argued, therefore, that the long post-war period of high demand simply reinforced a deep-seated 'cultural' resistance to change and efficiency on the shop floor.

While there is considerable room for argument about the causes of low productivity, its consequences are relatively unambiguous. It explains why British industry's unit costs and prices tend to rise faster than those of our major competitors. The problem is not that British trade union leaders and shop stewards are so much greedier than their foreign counterparts. Indeed, measured by total hourly wage costs, British labour is now one of the least expensive within the OECD area. A relatively slow rise in productivity, however, means that increases in wage costs are more likely to have an inflationary effect on unit costs, which will in turn damage industrial competitiveness (see Table 12).

Table 12

Unit labour costs, 1970–75

	Per cent increase in hourly wages (own currency)	Per cent increase in output per man hour	Per cent rise in unit labour costs (own currency)
Belgium	125	28	75
UK	120	15	91
France	102	15	76
Germany	86	29	44
Italy	170	27	112
Japan	148	24	99
Netherlands	108	26	64
Sweden	97	24	58
USA	48	10	34

Source: US Bureau of Labor Statistics.

Productivity performance is a strategic influence on international competitiveness. One recent survey of British industrial growth over the period 1950–73 found a strong association between increases in exports and higher rates of output, employment and productivity growth. Those industries whose productivity is increasing most rapidly are able to remain internationally competitive and enjoy higher rates of export growth which, in turn, raises growth rates of output and employment.[28]

In general, however, the productivity performance of most British manufacturing industries has been relatively poor. Panic, for example, has estimated that between 1954 and 1972, labour productivity in West German manufacturing industry as a whole increased by an average of 4·6 per cent a year, compared with 2·9 per cent in Britain.[29] Over the same period the proportion of total manufacturing output exported increased much faster in Germany (from 14·3 to 24·3 per cent) than in Britain (13·6 to 15·2 per cent). This unsatisfactory performance has been reflected in the declining share of British goods in world exports of manufactures. In 1960 Britain accounted for 15·3 per cent of this trade; by 1974, however, Britain's share had fallen to 8·3 per cent, despite the devaluation of sterling. This deteriorating export performance in effect constitutes a balance of payments constraint on growth and full employment. Since 1966 successive governments have sought to keep the growth of domestic demand below the growth of Britain's productive potential so as to 'make room' for a switch of resources into exports and investment. All that the strategy has succeeded in doing, however, is to weaken further the manufacturing sector. Such productivity growth as there has been has occurred against a background of slow output growth. In 1967–73 industrial output per head rose on average about 4 per cent a year, while total industrial output increased by an average of only 2·5 per cent a year. As a result employment in the production industries fell steadily throughout this period. In Panic's words: 'In conditions of prolonged under-utilization of capacity, firms will cut any costs in order to survive (hence the reduction in their labour force), and they will certainly see no reason to *expand* their productive capacity.'[30] The obvious danger is that the long period of depressed demand has permanently weakened the ability of British industry to respond to an expansion of demand. If this has indeed happened then any attempt to restore full employment through demand management will soon founder on a growing balance of payments constraint. Is this process reversible, or is Britain locked into a downward spiral of 'de-industrialization'?

The de-industrialization syndrome

In 1975 Bacon and Eltis published their now well-known thesis that the British economy has 'too few producers'. They argued that the improved productivity performance of 1967–73 *could* have had a positive effect on the overall rate of growth. The fact that it merely resulted in a higher level of unemployment can be explained in terms of a major structural change in the economy. Bacon and Eltis point out that between 1961 and 1974 employment in the 'non-market' sector of the economy increased by over one-third relative to employment in the 'market' sector. The 'market' sector represents the productive base of the economy and as such generates the marketable goods and services from which total consumption, investment and exports must be financed. The 'non-market' sector, by contrast, is composed almost exclusively of public services which, while they may be eminently desirable, contribute nothing to the process of wealth-creation. Public services are literally parasitic on the market sector. Bacon and Eltis maintain that in Britain the non-market sector has expanded too rapidly in relation to the market sector's capacity to support it, with the result that there has been a massive squeeze on resources:

> With more workers employed outside industry, more industrial production will be required for the consumption of those who have played no direct part in producing it. Similarly, more investment outside industry will be needed, and the capital goods will all have to be taken from the output of the industrial sector itself. It must follow that less industrial production will be available for investment and consumption by those who actually produce it or that all the extra goods the non-industrialists require will have to be imported. All these needs can, of course, be met if industrial production can be increased rapidly, but . . . in Britain the rate of growth of industrial production was exceedingly slow.[31]

Consequently, the rapid growth of non-industrial employment has taken resources away from the balance of payments and industrial investment.

The effects of this squeeze have been cumulative because up to 1975 non-industrial employment increased through recessions and booms, thereby reducing the capacity of the industrial sector to meet all the demands placed upon it. Since public service employment must be financed through taxation, another important side-effect of this over-rapid expansion has been a growing tax burden on industrial workers and a consequent increase in trade union militancy. But the real damage can be seen in the rapid deterioration of the 'full employment' balance of payments and the growth of structural unemployment. Since 1964 attempts by successive governments to expand aggregate demand and move towards full employment have resulted in vast and growing balance of payments deficits which have quickly brought a halt to expansion. Import penetration, however, has remained on a strong upward trend, and the ability of British industry to fend off foreign competition has steadily declined. Currency depreciation has failed to reverse the trend because devaluation in itself cannot cure the underlying structural weaknesses of the economy. The capacity of the market sector has contracted because profits and investment have been squeezed by the claims of the public service sector, and if productivity continues to rise faster than output then industrial employment must fall. The lack of sufficient industrial plant to provide work for more than a falling proportion of the labour force implies a growing problem of structural unemployment. In Friedman's terminology, the natural rate of unemployment has increased but governments have tried to counteract this trend by creating even more jobs in the public sector. This strategy has not only given a further twist to the downward spiral of de-industrialization but has caused accelerating inflation, to which the response has been an increasingly draconic regulation of wage bargaining. In a nutshell, therefore, Bacon and Eltis deny that low productivity is at the root of Britain's economic problem. The real cause of our difficulties is that such productivity growth as we had up to 1974 merely caused more redundancies and increasing structural unemployment in the market sector.

The Bacon and Eltis thesis of cumulative de-industrialization is partly supported by our own conclusions concerning the recent growth of structural unemployment in Britain. It suggests that higher productivity alone will not solve Britain's economic problems. What is needed is a major increase in market sector investment so that the productive potential of employees in this sector can be enhanced. Without such investment higher productivity will simply cause more unemployment. The projected increase in investment can only be financed if the non-market sector is prevented from expanding any further. In macro-economic terms, this strategy implies severe restrictions on public spending and a much more favourable attitude to profits. It also implies that the very low level of *capital* productivity in Britain must be raised. But this in turn is a function not only of the *level* and *quality* of investment but also of the *efficiency* with which it is used. It was argued in the preceding section, however, that the inefficient use of capital equipment is as much a behavioural as an economic problem and is therefore unlikely to be resolved quickly. Moreover, there is little evidence to support the argument that 'excessive' public spending and a large public sector borrowing requirement have 'crowded out' the private investor and thereby starved industry of financial resources. On the contrary, it may well be that governments have simply made use of loanable funds which would otherwise have remained idle.

A more fundamental question arising from the Bacon and Eltis hypothesis is *why* the structural shift in employment has occurred. Have successive governments deliberately created more and better public services in response to the perceived needs of the electorate? Or have they simply absorbed a large proportion of the labour which has been either 'shaken out' or 'shut out' of the market sector by the combination of faster productivity growth and inadequate demand? If the public service sector has simply acted as a 'sponge', soaking up redundant labour which would otherwise have been unemployed, it can hardly be blamed for the cumulative spiral of de-industrialization. Indeed, it may simply have siphoned off large sums of public money which would otherwise have been spent on unemployment benefit.

A balance of payments constraint?

Bacon and Eltis's central thesis has been attacked by Thirlwall, who argues that industrial output could not have risen as fast as productivity growth, even if employment in the non-market sector had not increased, because of a fundamental balance of payments constraint. If output *had* grown at the same rate as productivity, the consequences for the balance of payments would have been devastating because of the volume of imports which this expansion of demand would have sucked in.[32] It is generally accepted that since the 1950s there has been a steady, and in recent years accelerating, increase in Britain's marginal propensity to import manufactured goods. Between 1970 and 1975 the annual level of manufactured imports rose by 88 per cent in value terms; by contrast the index of domestic manufactured output rose by only 1·4 per cent. The share of finished and semi-finished manufactured goods in total imports rose from 33 per cent in 1962 to 56 per cent in 1973.[33] Imports of manufactured goods (unlike those of raw materials) reflect a *replacement* of domestic output by foreign products and as such have direct implications for the level of employment.

Why has import penetration grown so rapidly in recent years? One explanation is that imports of manufactured goods are more responsive to income changes in Britain than in comparable industrial countries. It has been estimated that Britain's income elasticity of demand for imports is about 1·6 and the world income elasticity of demand for British exports is about unity. Thus an annual rate of, say, 4 per cent output growth in Britain would, other things being equal, generate a 6·4 per cent growth of imports and a 4 per cent growth of exports. Thirlwall's estimates suggest that there are no fewer than thirty manufacturing industries (including motor vehicles, textiles and domestic electrical appliances) which have an income elasticity of demand for imports in excess of *two*. In other words, this suggests that for every 1 per cent increase in real incomes in the UK, there is a two-fold increase in the value of imported manufactures in this group of industries. The higher income elasticity value for Britain can be explained in terms of inadequate productive capacity in the manufacturing sector. Whenever domestic demand has been increased manufactured imports have grown rapidly and, equally important, have shown no tendency to decline during subsequent periods of demand restriction. Nor, in general, has currency depreciation affected the underlying trend. If a balance of payments constraint is to be removed by devaluation, then both import and export demand and supply *elasticities* must be sensitive enough to effect a real shift of resources into import substitution and export growth.[34] If, however, imports are price-inelastic, or if exporters respond to devaluation by simply increasing their profit margins, the necessary shift is unlikely to occur. Inelasticities of export supply and import demand account for the failure of successive devaluations to effect a fundamental improvement in Britain's balance of payments. Over the decade 1967–77 the price-quality mix of manufactured imports increased, while comparisons of export-import unit values suggest that Britain is gradually being forced out of the market for higher quality, relatively expensive manufactured goods.[35]

How does the theory of a balance of payments constraint relate to our previous conclusions about low productivity and de-industrialization? The Bacon and Eltis emphasis on Britain's declining manufacturing base is clearly relevant in so far as it accounts for the failure of devaluation to encourage either widespread import-substitution or a major expansion in exporting capacity. Thus the OECD has recently argued that if full employment is to be restored, Britain will need to spend an additional 2·5 per cent of its GDP on investment in manufacturing industry – presumably at the expense of public service investment.[36]

It is by no means certain, however, that the market sector *has* been starved of either manpower or investment by the non-market sector. A major investment boom in manufacturing will only occur in response to a high level of demand, sustainable over several years, and will in addition require a much greater return on whatever funds are invested. This means that industry will have to use its existing resources more efficiently, which in turn implies a massive attack on low productivity. Productivity is a major factor in international competitiveness in so far as it determines the behaviour of unit costs and therefore prices. The outlines of a vicious circle should by now be clear. Productive capacity has grown too slowly in relation to the periodic expansion of domestic demand because new investment has been unattractive. The main reason why investment has been inadequate is that the return to the investor is too low, which in turn reflects widespread inefficiency in the use of existing resources. Low productivity has inflated unit costs and prices which, although partly offset by currency depreciation, has in turn weakened the balance of payments. Consequently the manufacturing base is less and less able to absorb even a modest expansion of aggregate demand and import penetration has increased. Since the disastrous 'Barber boom' of 1972–3, when a 6 per cent rise in GDP generated a 30 per cent increase in manufactured imports, domestic demand has been under severe restraint. Yet this in turn has discouraged any further growth in productive capacity, so that despite the massive devaluation of 1976 the recession has left the economy in no better position to cope with future increases in demand.

If this analysis is correct, the only way of restoring full employment must be through a radical improvement in Britain's export performance. Some economists argue that this will require – among other things – another major devaluation. Others maintain that the key to reducing unemployment lies in the introduction of import controls. With a system of import controls, domestic demand could be expanded without running up against the balance of payments constraint. The various options for policy-makers will be discussed in Chapter Five. It can, however, be argued that it is no longer realistic for governments to formulate strategies which assume that full employment will *ever* be restored, and that the critical factor is not so much the balance of payments constraint on growth but rather the projected divergence between the supply of labour and the demand for it. We are, it is said, moving inexorably towards a situation in which fewer people will need to be at work in order to produce a given quantity of goods and services. Let us now examine this view.

Short-term and long-term prospects

There can be little doubt that if the relationship between output, employment and productivity which held in the recessions of 1966–7 and 1970–71 had re-emerged during the most recent recession, the level of unemployment would have been considerably higher at the trough of the cycle than it actually was. Conversely, it would have responded more rapidly to the modest upturn in activity which began in 1978. The fact that employment did not fall as fast as output may be attributed partly to the government's policy of subsidizing jobs and partly to the growing legal and financial constraints on mass redundancy. Whatever the reasons for this trend, however, at least one result must be self-evident. When the next major upswing *does* arrive, the effect on the aggregate level of unemployment will not be dramatic because many employers will undoubtedly be able to expand their output from roughly the same labour force. In December 1976, for example, the National Institute of Economic and Social Research (NIESR) conducted a survey of spare capacity among manufacturing firms and found that output could have been increased by an average of 7 per cent with *no* additional overtime or labour. The same firms reported that they could achieve a further average increase in output of 12 per cent *with* additional overtime but *no* extra labour. A shift towards more capital-intensive production methods, or simply an autonomous improvement in organizational efficiency, would have the same effect. The NIESR survey concluded that the evidence pointed to a 'surprisingly large degree of inefficiency' in the use of labour and inferred that in many cases employers would not recruit more manpower until the existing margin of slack had been fully used up.[37]

But while there is relatively little disagreement about the immediate trend in unemployment, the longer-term prospects are more problematic. Projections of the future labour force by the Department of Employment suggest that over the period 1977–91 it will increase by 2·2 million (or 8·4 per cent), or by about 146,000 a year. Much of this growth, however, may well occur in the period up to 1985 when the annual average rate of increase is projected at 176,000. This reflects both a relatively high rate of entry into the labour market by young people and a continued rise in the activity rate among married women. The projections for school-leavers should be reasonably accurate since they reflect known demographic trends in the early 1960s. They

88

suggest that school-leaver entry will peak in 1982 and then gradually decline as the falling birth rates of the late 1960s and early 1970s begin to be felt. The forecast for married women may be somewhat less reliable since it critically depends on an assumed activity rate. The Department suggests that the activity rate of this group will continue to rise, but at a slower rate than in the early 1970s. If, however, there was *no* increase in this rate, the overall growth in the labour force would be nearly 40 per cent less than the projected figure.[38] Clearly much will depend on the rate at which service employment, both public and private, continues to expand; the faster the rate, the more likely it is to stimulate a corresponding increase in the number of women seeking jobs (including part-time jobs) in this sector.

If unemployment is to be reduced over the next few years, then output must expand fast enough to absorb existing spare capacity. Output must also grow faster than productivity so that new entrants into the labour market as well as some of those who are currently out of work can be employed. The Manpower Services Commission, for example, has constructed a 'job gap curve' which suggests that 1·34 million additional jobs would be needed to reduce aggregate registered unemployment to 800,000 by 1981. A more modest target of 1·2 million unemployed would still require an extra 800,000 jobs.[39] The Commission has argued that even the more ambitious of these targets is 'not an impossible task in relation to past performance', and quotes the rate of job creation achieved in 1972 (50,000 per month) in support of its conclusion. It is now generally agreed, however, that the expansion of demand achieved in 1972 was far too rapid to be sustained for long and, leaving aside the consequences for inflation and the balance of payments, the rate of growth quickly ground to a halt in 1973 as production bottlenecks and shortages of labour appeared. The Commission's target would require output to expand on average by 5 per cent a year in 1977–81 and productivity to increase by 3 per cent a year over the same period. A significant growth in manufacturing as well as service employment would also be needed if the rate of male and school-leaver unemployment was to be reduced. But it seems unlikely that any of these conditions will be met.

Forecasting economic growth rates for the next decade is, of course, fraught with uncertainties. Much will depend on the rate at which world trade expands and on the international rate of inflation. Most forecasters, however, see no reason why the British economy (with or without North Sea oil) should grow at a rate significantly above its long-term trend rate of about 2·5 per cent a year. The implications for the level of unemployment are by no means clear, because of the problem of predicting the behaviour of both productivity and the balance of payments. Leicester, for example, has suggested that if the economy sustained a 'healthy' average GDP growth rate of 2·7 per cent a year up to 1991 and productivity rose by 2·5 per cent a year, only 800,000 jobs would be created over the entire period. Given the projected growth of the labour supply, and assuming no change in working hours, this would mean a steep rise in unemployment to 2·9 million by 1986 and 3·3 million by 1991.[40] Pessimistic assumptions about the balance of payments produce equally pessimistic predictions about unemployment. The revenue from North Sea oil should, of course, bring the balance of payments into a strong surplus position during the 1980s. But this may only serve to conceal temporarily the underlying decline in the productive base of the economy. If manufactured imports continue to increase at their recent rate there will be a severe loss of jobs in manufacturing industry which will be only partially offset by further expansion in the service sector. Thus the Cambridge Economic Policy Group has predicted that if present policies are continued unemployment could reach 4·5 million by 1990. In their view this outcome can only be avoided by a massive devaluation or, preferably, by import controls.[41]

Whether the balance of payments constraint on the British economy grows worse or not, it is likely that Britain, along with most other advanced industrial countries, will experience a continuing decline in manufacturing employment and a steady increase in service employment over the next decade or so. This trend is already well established. In 1960 a total of 39·5 per cent of workers in the enlarged Common Market area were in service employment. By 1973 this proportion had risen to 47·6 per cent and in certain countries (Britain, Holland, Belgium and Denmark) the share of service employment was well over 50 per cent. This is, of course, a trend common to all 'post-industrial' societies. On the one hand it probably reflects a general demand for more extensive public (non-market) services, for example in education, health and social care. In Britain this demand may, as Bacon and Eltis argue, have been allowed to expand too quickly relative to the capacity of the industrial sector to support it and as a consequence may have to be restrained in the future. But, on the other hand, it also reflects the increasing importance of private (market) services, such as finance, leisure and commerce, in societies where fewer people need to be employed in the physical production of goods. These services can properly be regarded as wealth-creating and indeed in recent years have made a very important contribution to Britain's balance of payments. We must also reiterate that since 1971 employment in the market service in Britain has increased much more rapidly than in the non-market sector. But it would be misleading to conclude that in general the service sector has grown at the *expense* of industrial employment. In many European countries (excluding Britain and Sweden), service employment has certainly increased but employment in the primary sector (mainly agriculture) has fallen much more sharply than it has in industry.[42]

Nevertheless there seems to have been an autonomous contraction in certain types of manufacturing employment which is likely to continue over the next two decades and may even accelerate. In Britain the steady loss of jobs in industries such as textiles, steel, shipbuilding, coal and various kinds of engineering is a familiar story. But the same trend is clearly visible in every other advanced industrial country, including Japan. Between 1970 and 1978 employment in Japanese manufacturing industry as a whole fell by over 10 per cent, and in certain sectors (textiles and shipbuilding) the decline was much more rapid. While the recent recession obviously accounts for some of this erosion, even the most optimistic Japanese forecasts suggest that by 1990 only a quarter of the labour force will be employed in manufacturing. Employment in the service sector, by contrast, is expected to increase rapidly and indeed it will need to do so if Japan's growing unemployment problem is to be solved.[43] Two important developments help to explain this general trend. Firstly, manufacturing industry in all the advanced industrial countries is becoming more capital-intensive and the impending development of micro-process technology is likely to accelerate this trend. Secondly, some of the oldest industries in the Western world have in recent years been subject to intense competition from newly industrializing countries in Asia, South America and southern Europe. Imports from these countries of clothing, leather goods, footwear, textiles and electrical machinery have all increased rapidly since the 1960s, and indeed have already given rise to certain protectionist measures in the USA and Western Europe. The structure of relative labour costs has, however, given the newly industrializing countries a decisive advantage and in the long term it will almost certainly accelerate the movement of labour out of basic manufacturing employment in the old-established industrial countries.[44]

Where will this labour go and how, in addition, will the new entrants to the labour market be employed? Countries like Japan and West Germany, where the growth of service employment started relatively late, may be in a stronger position than those such as Britain or the USA where services have been expanding rapidly for many years. In Britain one can no longer assume that *public* service employment will continue to expand at its pre-1974 rate, if only because of the implications for government spending and taxation. Demographic trends are also likely to be an important influence in this field. From the mid-1980s onwards, fewer and fewer children will be entering the education system so that further growth in education services is likely to be modest. Department of Employment projections suggest that there will be some increase in the number of students going into further full-time education up to 1986, but even if this happens (and there is little sign of it yet) it will only have a marginal effect on the labour force. At the other end of the age-scale, the number of people reaching retirement age will be below average up to 1982 because of the low birth-rates during the First World War. The post-1918 'bulge' will temporarily increase those of retirement age in the mid-1980s, but the sharp and continuing fall in birth rates between 1920 and 1940 means that fewer and fewer people will be retiring each year from the late 1980s onwards. On the basis of these trends it would be unrealistic to assume that there will be a major increase in the demand for health and social services from the old, unless of course the projected mortality rate turns out to be too high. Official forecasts of medium-term prospects in housing are also gloomy in their implications for employment. Virtually all the relevant variables point towards less new building in both the public and the private sectors.[45]

Employment in the private service sector and perhaps in capital-intensive industries such as electronics will probably continue to grow, however, although the rate of growth *may* be more modest than in recent years. A reduction in working hours, for example, should see a further growth in demand for leisure services, although this will also depend on how fast real incomes grow. Further growth in information services should also be anticipated. The message for policy-makers, however, is that the demand for labour will become increasingly selective and particularist in character. Certain types of skilled labour will continue to be in short supply, especially in the nascent but potentially enormous micro-electronics market. Indeed the skill content of labour in the most important growth industries will almost certainly increase. This has clear implications for the level and character of unemployment in Britain over the next decade. Unless current forecasts of the overall growth of the economy are unduly pessimistic, one can easily foresee that the shut-out of the unqualified young will continue, especially among men. Leicester, for example, has predicted that unemployment in the under-20 age group will remain at its present rate throughout the 1980s, which in the peak entry years of 1983–5 would mean that about half a million teenagers would be out of work. Many of these may not be able to get a job of any kind when they leave school and it will thus be even more difficult to find employment for them in subsequent years. Conversely, a continuing shake-out of labour from the manufacturing sector will throw on to the market a large number of men with a highly specific and thus largely untransferable experience of work.[46] These projected developments will pose a real challenge to the ingenuity of labour market policy-makers over the next few years.

Summary

There is little point in arguing that unemployment should be reduced to its pre-1966 level since this is plainly impossible. Indeed, in view of the probability that employment in the 1948–66 period was *over*-full, it could well be argued that a policy of bringing unemployment back to this level would not in any case be desirable. But at what level of unemployment should we now regard the economy as fully employed? In its 1977 review, the NIESR suggested that if 1·5 per cent (350,000) represented full employment up to 1966, a level of 1·9 to 2·4 per cent (450–550,000) might represent full employment in the late 1970s. In the light of the argument presented above, however, this estimate seems unduly optimistic. During the 1970s the level of unemployment fell to half a million in only one year (1973) and was associated with acute and widespread shortages of labour and other production bottlenecks.[47] It seems that employment was once again over-full, but at a somewhat higher level than in the pre-1966 period. An alternative approach would be to argue that in 1972–3 the government's excessive stimulation of demand pushed unemployment below its natural rate and thereby stimulated the rapid inflation of 1974–5, but it is impossible, in view of the limitations of the official data, to quantify the natural rate. Finally, the government itself appears, at the time of writing, to have abandoned the idea of setting a target level to which it believes unemployment can be reduced. Up to 1976 ministers were talking in terms of bringing unemployment down to 700,000 by 1979, but after the financial crisis of 1976 this target was quietly dropped and no realistic alternative has yet been suggested. In 1977 the Manpower Services Commission seemed to be thinking in terms of a target figure of 800,000 unemployed by 1981, but even this level will require a rate of job creation which the economy cannot on present trends even begin to sustain. If ministers know what 'full employment' now means in terms of an unemployment percentage (which is very doubtful), they are evidently determined not to publicize it.

Since the late 1960s successive governments have been forced to accept that they can no longer set their own full employment target which 'trades off' other macro-economic objectives. The rise in the natural rate of unemployment and the escalation of inflationary expectations have led to a sharp and probably permanent deterioration in the relationship between inflation and unemployment. It would probably be going too far to say that the Phillips Curve no longer exists, but its attractions for policy-makers have obviously disappeared. The Keynesian approach is also fraught with difficulties in so far as its prescription for achieving full employment – appropriate enough in the conditions of the 1930s – could also be associated with a further outbreak of rapid inflation. Its emphasis on restoring real wages to their equilibrium level through an increase in aggregate demand (which must, presumably, be reinforced by a tough incomes policy) is on recent evidence unlikely to elicit the support of the trade unions for more than a very limited period. Consequently the government has been forced to abandon any pretence of having a full employment policy *per se*. The hope is that if wage restraint continues, if the growth of the money supply is firmly controlled, if investment in manufacturing industry revives, if the continued growth of public service employment is curtailed and if world trade expands faster than it has done in recent years, then unemployment will *eventually* fall, but when and by how much remains problematic.

Unfortunately for policy-makers the situation may well get worse over the next decade. Unless the economy expands at a much higher average rate than it has ever sustained before, the demand for labour will not match the supply. Manufacturing industry, both in Britain and in other advanced countries, will require less and less labour. In Britain, however, the fall in employment may well accelerate if the balance of payments constraint on growth continues to tighten. Although there is a growing structural element in Britain's overall unemployment problem, it would be absurd not to recognize the importance of the low level of demand for goods and services in the economy. But, in the words of the NIESR, 'the long-standing problem of how to stimulate demand through investment and exports, rather than through consumption, remains'.[48] Even if import controls are adopted or the currency is allowed to depreciate, the balance of payments constraint will not be eased until there is a major improvement in industrial productivity. Such an improvement is, however, likely to be achieved by a more efficient use of existing manpower resources, and the short-term prospects for additional job-creation in the industrial sector seem very bleak.[49] In theory, of course, the growing manpower surplus could be absorbed by a sustained increase in those forms of employment which demand little new capital but a good deal of labour. Most public service employment would fall into this category. But this form of job creation is ultimately tax-dependent and as such implies a growing squeeze on the incomes of those in 'self-financing' employment. The implications of such a squeeze for inflation, the balance of payments and the capacity of both the industrial and private service sector to generate more wealth would hardly be consistent with a strategy aimed at reducing the level of unemployment.

The policies which might be consistent with such a strategy will be considered in the next chapter.

CHAPTER FIVE

Some Options for Policy-makers

> The old attitude was that unemployment was a tragedy, and so it was for many in the circumstances of 40 years ago. The new and hopeful attitude must be that unemployment is a necessary process in a changing economy, and that the role of the British government should not be to resist it by subsidizing outdated industry and encouraging workers to believe that all jobs are for life, but to smooth the paths of change in general and to help individuals adapt themselves to it.
>
> Arthur Seldon, 1975

Part of the solution to our current unemployment problem lies in a sustained expansion of economic activity. It follows that one of the major tasks facing all Western governments is to find a way of expanding demand without giving a new impetus to the inflationary spiral or imposing an intolerable strain on the balance of payments. So far, however, almost every government has given priority to reducing inflation, with the result that demand management policies have been generally restrictive and unemployment has remained at a relatively high level. In these circumstances it is hardly surprising that economists in the weaker industrial countries such as Britain have been looking for ways of breaking the link between aggregate demand and the balance of payments. One much-canvassed solution relies on the introduction of import controls which, it is said, will enable the government to increase demand without driving the balance of payments into deficit.

Do we need import controls?

The principal argument for import controls is that in theory they would give British manufacturing firms a secure and steadily expanding domestic market which would in turn facilitate a dramatic increase in production, employment and investment. Industrial growth would be freed from the balance of payments constraint and the long decline in the manufacturing base of the economy would be reversed. In Godley's words: 'The growth of imports is held down to what can be financed from export earnings while the growth of home demand is adjusted, via tax rates and public spending, to the rate at which supply can be expanded.'[1] It is often pointed out that temporary, selective quotas on imports are permitted under the General Agreement of Tariffs and Trade (GATT) and in Britain's case the principal candidates for quotas would include a number of consumer goods industries, for example, motorcars and components and electronic equipment. Action in these sectors would not in fact constitute a radical departure for policy-makers in Britain, since the textile and coal industries have long been protected by a complex structure of import controls and production subsidies. The presumption must be that a period of protection would put manufacturing firms in a much better position to combat foreign competition when the import controls were eventually dismantled.

This is a complex issue, but the protectionist solution seems to have several major weaknesses. First and foremost it is not immediately obvious that greater protection will give the British government the necessary freedom to expand aggregate demand and reduce unemployment. The idea of selective import controls is appealing in so far as it seems to offer a means of avoiding a general tariff war with our major trading partners. Such controls have been applied to a number of declining industries in Britain and other Western countries for several years and the most that can be said is that they have made the process of decline somewhat less uncomfortable than it might otherwise have been. Protectionists would, however, hasten to point out that the real threat of higher import penetration lies not so much in these traditionally vulnerable sectors as in the consumer goods industries which have been much more closely associated with postwar economic growth. The principal source of import penetration in this sector is, of course, Japan. In recent years almost every

Western country has experienced in varying degrees the impact of Japanese competition in motor vehicles, motorcycles, television sets, transistor radios and a range of other consumer durables. The response so far has consisted of a series of 'voluntary restraint' agreements negotiated with the Japanese on an industry-by-industry basis. The problem is that the selective approach permits the Japanese to switch their efforts to those industries (such as commercial vehicles and video-recorders) which are not yet covered by voluntary import quotas. One can only conclude that if protection against Japan is to be effective it can hardly be selective. But if quotas were applied in every sector of European manufacturing industry it would presumably encourage the Japanese to make heavier inroads into Western Europe's own overseas export markets. It might also lead to a general re-alignment in exchange rates which would restore Japan's competitive advantage. To the extent that this happened, the balance of trade advantages from protection would be offset. In Britain's case, therefore, the balance of payments constraint would not disappear.

Let us suppose, however, that the adoption of more widespread import quotas and tariffs in Britain did *not* provoke widespread retaliation. Would protectionism enable British industry to break out of the downward spiral of low investment, low productivity and low output? Would it encourage British export industries to improve their performance and increase their share of world trade? It is not immediately obvious that it would. One reason for the balance of payments constraint on growth is, quite simply, that British industry has in the past reacted too slowly to the changing pattern of international competition. Import controls might actually encourage businessmen and trade union leaders alike to become even more inward-looking and thus more dependent on protection. They might also help to prop up inefficient producers who have no real future, thereby preserving uneconomic jobs and inhibiting structural change. In Corden's words: 'A policy that is essentially conservative in nature is not likely to foster change and growth. If everyone is assured that his slice of the cake will not be allowed to fall very much in absolute amount, the total cake is less likely to grow.'[2] If controls and quotas were applied to all imports except food and raw materials, there would be widespread shortages of consumer goods, machinery and equipment, leading to a *fall* in output. Protectionists would argue that these shortages should eventually be corrected by import substitution. The problem is that the British economy is now so dependent on imported manufactures that the volume of investment required to replace them by domestic output would be enormous. There is in fact nothing in the post-war record of the British economy which suggests that protection alone would enable it to achieve and sustain the rates of output, investment and productivity growth which the protectionists say are essential if full employment is to be restored.

Do we need an incomes policy?

A much more conventional prescription for reducing unemployment is based on the assumption that the rate of inflation is a major influence on the level of unemployment. Since wages are a key factor in inflation, an incomes policy must be an essential part of any strategy against unemployment. The argument is valid to the extent that an incomes policy can help to adjust real wages to their equilibrium level. Opponents of an incomes policy, however, would reply that on the rare occasions when incomes policy has more or less succeeded, the real reason for its apparent effectiveness may be found in the restriction of the money supply by the authorities. They would further argue that because all incomes policies interfere with the structure of relativities and differentials, they eventually provoke a strong reaction from the trade unions. These wage 'explosions' tend to wipe out any 'gains' which may have been achieved over the previous incomes policy cycle and leave wage aspirations higher than they were before.

These are powerful objections but, if they are accepted as conclusive, policy-makers are left with a difficult choice. The apparent collapse of the Phillips Curve means that unemployment (in so far as it can be regarded as a proxy for aggregate demand) is an ineffective weapon against inflation. Yet inflation, by pushing up costs and prices in Britain relative to those of our major competitors, tightens the balance of payments constraint on growth and thereby increases unemployment. In the absence of an incomes policy, the only short-term solution would be to allow excessive domestic inflation to be 'corrected' by currency depreciation which, by reducing real incomes, might simply provoke further wage inflation. A strategy which combined strict control of the money supply with free collective bargaining could not, one suspects, be sustained for very long, particularly if it encountered strong opposition from the most powerful bargaining groups in the public sector. We are left with the protectionist argument that since real wages are bound to rise anyway, the only sensible response is for governments to increase output (i.e. real national incomes) by stimulating demand. This would only work, however, if protection succeeded in removing the balance of payments constraint on domestic growth and, as we argue above, this is by no means certain.

One important element in the balance of payments constraint, however, is the low average level of productivity in British industry. Is there any action which the government could take in order to encourage productivity growth? Two suggestions are made in the course of this chapter, first that the standard working week could be reduced to 37 or 35 hours, and second that the government could encourage manpower planning among public and private employers alike. The problem here is that a strategy for increasing productivity is not necessarily consistent, at least in the short term, with a strategy for reducing unemployment. Indeed, the success of the government's job-preserving measures during 1975–7 may well account for the concurrent stagnation in productivity. Common sense suggests that if manpower is being used inefficiently, the most effective way of inducing employers to improve productivity is not to reduce labour costs (as employment subsidies do) but to make labour more expensive relative to capital. Unfortunately, experience suggests that the relationship between rising labour costs and productivity is not straightforward. In labour-intensive industries, a sharp rise in wage costs may lead to some shake-out at the margin, but the experience of 1974–6 suggests that it is more likely to encourage a shut-out of new labour. This may, of course, simply reflect the job-preserving bias of labour market policy. Yet the persistence of high levels of overtime even at the trough of the recent recession suggests that inefficient working practices may have become institutionalized and thus largely resistant to movements in relative costs. To the extent that this is true it suggests that the task of improving productivity is likely to be longer and more difficult than is often imagined, and will require a wide range of supportive measures by the government.

While there is no space here to discuss these measures in depth, we may suggest that incomes policy is by no means irrelevant in this context. During the late 1960s incomes policy was used, with some success, to stimulate bargaining over efficiency issues at company and plant level. The experience of productivity bargaining suggests that at least some of the sources of low productivity can be tackled through joint action in the workplace. The policy had many weaknesses, but it did at least fix the attention of negotiators on the fundamental relationship between real incomes, efficiency and output. Since then, however, the concept of productivity bargaining has fallen into disrepute. Successive governments have (mistakenly) chosen to believe that most productivity agreements were phoney, while many trade unionists have resisted measures which seem designed to reduce employment opportunities. But productivity bargaining is still relevant in so far as it recognizes the importance of behavioural and institutional factors in low productivity and rightly assumes that many of these can only be removed by negotiation and agreement in the workplace.

Incomes policy could be used as a vehicle for other equally desirable changes in the wage bargaining system. It was argued in Chapter Four that the fragmented structure of the British system of wage bargaining enables many negotiators to discount the macro-economic implications of their decisions. The gradual spread of workplace bargaining in recent years has if anything sharpened the dichotomy between the rational and legitimate aspirations of negotiators and the broader, equally rational needs of the economy. In Blackaby's words:

The requirement for policy is to try to find institutional changes which, as it were, bring the two rationalities closer together. The changes have to make more transparent the macro-economic consequences of the sum total of individual negotiating decisions, in such a way that those individual decisions are themselves affected.[3]

Blackaby has therefore suggested three reforms which should help to achieve this objective. Firstly, he proposes that each year the government, the TUC and the CBI should try to reach an agreement not only on the desirable norm for wage settlements, but also on broader economic and social priorities. Secondly, he suggests that all major negotiations in both the public and private sectors should move towards a common settlement date. Thirdly, he advocates the re-establishment of a national arbitral body (along the lines of the former Prices and Incomes Board) so that above-the-norm wage claims could be evaluated according to agreed criteria. While all these proposals are likely to encounter powerful opposition – mainly, one suspects, from trade unionists who will see them as a direct attack on their own independence – it must surely be recognized that sooner or later the old belief that collective bargaining can and should be entirely free of government influence will have to be abandoned. Blackaby's proposals represent three essential steps towards the permanent regulation of wage bargaining, which must in turn be regarded as an essential part of any strategy designed to avoid higher unemployment.

The main contribution which an incomes policy can make towards reducing unemployment lies in helping to create a climate of opinion on the shop floor which is more favourable to higher productivity. Incomes policy alone, however, will not be enough to bring about the requisite changes. The Callaghan government seems to have accepted the nominally right-wing argument that investment in the market sector of the economy will not increase unless the claims of the non-market sector are held down and the burden of personal and corporate taxation is reduced. This might mean, for example, that all classes of investment should receive a 100-per-cent tax depreciation allowance, or that tax reliefs on changes in stock values should be improved, or that price and dividend controls should be abolished. A strong case can indeed be made for such a strategy but it must be admitted that it requires a degree of confidence in both the entrepreneurship of British managers and the cooperativeness of British trade unionists which would be hard to justify in the light of experience.

The Labour left argues, therefore, that the government itself must take the initiative in identifying key growth sectors and ensuring that they have an adequate supply of investment capital. The present government (1978) has adopted this approach, albeit with no great enthusiasm, and through the medium of the National Enterprise Board has channelled public funds into those industries and technologies which it believes will play a vital role in the future growth of the economy. The main problem with this kind of strategy is, however, the tendency in practice to invest heavily in declining industries and firms which get into difficulties, regardless of whether these firms have a real future or not. A policy of subsidizing production and employment can be defended on the grounds that it will help to prevent further short-term increases in unemployment, but this is not necessarily consistent with the pursuit of higher employment in the long term.

The subsidization of employment raises the broader issue of government intervention in the labour market. If our current unemployment problem was wholly attributable to deficient demand, the need for an active labour market policy would be more problematic. Our previous analysis, however, suggests that there is an important structural dimension which would, by definition, persist at a higher level of aggregate demand. Once it is recognized that the problem is partly structural in character, it is difficult to deny the need for more direct forms of intervention.

The rationale of labour market policy

The development of an active labour market policy has in recent years become an integral part of the present government's strategy for improving the performance of British industry. The White Paper on industrial regeneration (November 1976), for example, argued that skill shortages and low productivity were particularly serious constraints on economic growth which could be alleviated by government intervention. Since then the objectives of labour market policy have, under the aegis of the Manpower Services Commission, become more wide-ranging and now include, for example, the provision of those opportunities and services which any worker needs in order to lead a satisfying working life. The current interventionism stands in marked contrast to the traditional attitude of benign neglect. Until 1973 such legislation as there was reflected the labour market conditions of the pre-1966 period. The Redundancy Payments Act of 1965, for example, was based on the assumption that many kinds of labour were in short supply (a shortage induced partly by overmanning) and that mobility would be improved by giving redundant workers financial compensation for the loss of their jobs. The role of training in achieving a better match between supply and demand was also recognized in the Industrial Training Act of 1964, but again the underlying philosophy of the Act was essentially voluntarist in so far as it assumed that employers would increase their training efforts if given sufficient financial incentive to do so. By the early 1970s, however, it was becoming clear that the assumptions implicit in these two Acts were no longer valid. Voluntary training had not corrected even the most obvious imbalances in the labour market and monetary compensation had not removed the fear of redundancy. As unemployment rapidly increased from 1974 onwards, the need for a more comprehensive approach to labour market policy was quickly recognized.

Even the most devoted admirer of the Manpower Services Commission could hardly deny that the rapid expansion of its activities since 1974 has largely been an *ad hoc* response to the trend in aggregate unemployment. The same could of course be said of some of the protective measures adopted in Western Europe as a whole since 1974, the only difference being that countries such as Sweden, West Germany and France have all had much more experience of active intervention in the labour market. In Britain the traditional emphasis on voluntary action has meant that a new framework of institutions geared to a different philosophy has had to be improvised almost from scratch, and in these circumstances it would be very surprising indeed if no mistakes had been made. A more general problem arising from the speed with which the current strategy has been put together is that of ensuring consistency with the existing framework of employment law. The Employment Protection Act of 1975 seeks, for example, to strengthen security of employment in various ways and explicitly recognizes that employees have 'property rights' in their jobs. While the principle of compensation for redundancy has been retained, the 1975 Act imposes an obligation on managements to consult with trade unions when redundancy situations arise and, by implication, to find alternative methods (including reduced hours or work-sharing) of dealing with a downturn of business. But while this approach can easily be justified on social grounds, it is not *necessarily* consistent with a policy of encouraging managers and trade unionists to respond to the pressures of structural and technological change. The problem is, of course, that politicians are naturally interested in measures which will make the aggregate unemployment figures look better than they would otherwise be. Such measures may be effective in the short term while seriously prejudicing longer-term objectives.

The potential conflict between short- and long-term policy objectives raises the fundamental question of what we should expect any labour market policy to achieve and how this policy should relate to the wider macro-economic strategy which the government is pursuing. There are different degrees of intervention in labour markets which may in turn be motivated by different economic philosophies. In its simplest form intervention may be aimed at removing the more conspicuous mismatches by, for example, increasing the supply of skilled workers and taking steps to improve labour mobility. Policies of this kind have long been regarded as a legitimate form of intervention even by the more dogmatic advocates of the 'free market'. Ever since the 1930s, however, some governments have felt it necessary to go further and *create* jobs, financed by their own tax revenues, for the specific purpose of putting at least some of the unemployed to work. In recent years this practice has become more widespread, but the principle of tax-financed job creation continues to arouse hostility in certain quarters, particularly from those who argue that it is simply a wasteful 'cosmetic'. A much more controversial form of intervention is designed to preserve jobs that would otherwise disappear. This strategy may also include measures such as the reduction of working hours and enforced early retirement, the purpose of which is to reduce the labour supply. In the rest of this chapter we shall analyse these forms of intervention and evaluate their relevance to the current and projected unemployment problem in Britain.

Improving the effectiveness of labour markets

It was pointed out in Chapter Three that the most persistent structural imbalance in the labour market is the shortage of various kinds of skilled workers and the oversupply of all kinds of unskilled labour. The shortcomings of the voluntarist approach to correcting this mismatch were recognized in 1972 with the establishment of the Training Opportunities Scheme (TOPS). The beneficiaries of TOPS are adults who need some form of training in order to take up new employment. When introduced, it was evisaged that TOPS would extend and broaden the training facilities already provided through the government's 'skill centres', and on paper the scheme has been a success. In 1976 nearly 90,000 people completed courses with TOPS, which was double the corresponding figure for 1974 and an even greater improvement on the early 1960s when barely 4,000 workers a year were passing through the government training centres.[4]

In reality this achievement may be less impressive than it appears. One major criterion of the success of TOPS-supported training is the extent to which those who complete courses are able to find jobs using their newly learned skills. In 1976 about 75 per cent of those who completed courses did so either in colleges of further education or in employers' own establishments, and the remaining 25 per cent went through the skill centres. The Manpower Services Commission's own figures, however, suggest that the job prospects of those workers from the skill centres were significantly better than those of the people who went through the other establishments. This may well reflect the different kinds of training offered in these institutions. Two-thirds of all the courses were concentrated in clerical, commercial and miscellaneous occupations, and only one-third in the traditional craft skills.[5] The policy of the MSC is to spread TOPS courses over all those occupations for which skilled or trained adults are most likely to be needed. While this is no doubt helpful to individuals who wish to improve their employment prospects it may not be in the longer-term interests of the economy as a whole. It is not difficult to identify certain key occupations in which there is a persistent shortage of new entrants at the present time. It is more difficult, but not impossible, to identify those occupations which are likely to expand over the next few years and which will require an adequate supply of workers with specific skills. By spreading its efforts over a wide area, the MSC may be neglecting to invest enough resources in those forms of training which are likely to yield the greatest long-term benefits to the economy. It also seems to be neglecting the needs of those skilled workers (predominantly male and middle-aged) who have been 'shaken out' of the older, declining manufacturing industries. It has been estimated that the proportion of redundant workers who are retrained is still only about 5 per cent. Since this problem is likely to grow over the next decade, the MSC may well have to change its present 'catch-all' strategy in favour of something more selective.

It may, however, be argued that the persistent and growing shortage of workers in many of the traditional craft occupations will not be remedied simply by training more of them. The problem is partly one of overcoming the resistance of trade unionists to the employment of workers who have acquired their skill under TOPS rather than through the traditional apprenticeship system. Yet this system has in recent years proved increasingly incapable of supplying industry, especially the engineering industry, with the skilled manpower it needs. A survey by the Engineering Industry Training Board found that between 1965–6 and 1973–4 the proportion of craftsmen in the industry's labour force fell from nearly 22 per cent (or 754,000) to less than 19 per cent (or 595,000). In 1972–3 alone about 72,400 people left or changed their jobs as craftsmen in the industry, and although the majority (about 50,000) went to craft jobs elsewhere in engineering, some 23,000 workers actually left the craft labour force. This would not have mattered too much if there had been a corresponding inflow of trainees to replace these losses, but in 1972–3 only 15,500 craftsmen completed their five-year apprenticeships, which was barely more than half the number who had entered apprentice training at the beginning of the course in 1968–9. In view of the fact that the apprenticeship system still supplies about 80 per cent of engineering craftsmen, the annual recruitment of first-year craft and technician apprentices would need to be around 27,000 simply in order to keep the craft labour force stable. Between 1971 and 1975, however, the intake was well below this figure, so that the shortage of engineering craftsmen can be expected to continue, at least for a few years.[6]

But why is the engineering industry incapable of retaining so large a proportion of its existing stock of fully trained and apprentice craftsmen? One reason which is often quoted is the squeeze on skilled workers' differentials which, it is said, has greatly reduced the financial incentive to enter or stay in craft occupations. There is certainly some evidence to support this argument. Overall, the differential between the average earnings of skilled time-workers (excluding overtime) and those of their semi-skilled colleagues fell from nearly 10 per cent in June 1970 to less than 4 per cent in June 1976. In some industries, particularly motor vehicles, the compression has been even more severe. Even skilled workers who are paid under incentive schemes have seen their differentials eroded, particularly in engineering.[7] Dissatisfaction with pay does not, however, provide a comprehensive explanation. A survey by the National Economic Development Organization (NEDO) of skilled engineers who left their employment in 1972–4 throws further light on why shortages of skilled labour have been getting worse in recent years. No less than 42 per cent of the sample who had left their jobs in engineering found employment outside the industry in which their skills were not required. The main reasons for this exodus included the lack of job security in the industry (redundancy), poor prospects for advancement, low pay and bad working conditions. The conclusions of the report are worth quoting:

Most craftsmen have invested several years in training, at considerable cost to themselves. In the past one thing skilled men possessed was relative security of tenure of what they considered to be their job property rights. Once the employer shakes them out, then they will look over the fence to see if the grass is greener there, and the other factors – pay, conditions and so on – will assume greater importance. If their skill can be considered an expendable commodity by the industry then they could reasonably, if reluctantly, consider it expendable to themselves. While some will always prefer to work in engineering, it may well be that many others will feel under no inclination to transfer their skills within the industry or wait until the industry feels able to require them again. It may make sense to abandon their skill and simply transfer to a job unrelated to their training and experience.[8]

The underlying lack of job security may also explain in part the determination of many craftsmen to preserve old-fashioned working practices which in turn contribute to the low level of labour productivity. The obvious answer is for managements to give their craftsmen higher pay and increased security of employment as a *quid pro quo* for their cooperation with measures to raise productivity. In many companies, however, such a strategy would have far-reaching industrial relations implications in so far as it would directly challenge the long-established trend towards uniformity of treatment for all work-groups.[9] Moreover, in view of the increasing competition from overseas which the engineering industry is likely to face over the next few years, it may be very difficult in practice for managements to give any guarantees of job security even if they wanted to. An alternative strategy, therefore, would be to abandon the approach to redundancy embodied in the 1965 Act. Britain is almost unique in its emphasis on lump sum redundancy payments which, furthermore, are related not to personal need but to the previous income, age and length of service of the worker. It would make much more sense to follow the example of countries such as Sweden and West Germany and place far more emphasis on the right of all redundant workers to retraining and redeployment without loss of earnings. Since redundancy will in all probability become more frequent over the next few years, it seems increasingly inappropriate to rely on the principle of indiscriminate, once-and-for-all cash payments to those affected.[10] More attention will have to be given to the problem of conserving and increasing the stock of skills in the economy and this can only be done through a much bigger investment in retraining facilities, even though it must be accepted that not every retrained worker can be guaranteed employment.

The other serious mismatch which we identified in Chapter Three concerns a small but growing minority of school-leavers who have in recent years found the task of getting and keeping a job increasingly difficult. What, if anything, can be done to reverse this trend? The evidence suggests that those EEC countries (for example, West Germany) which incorporate vocational preparation into the educational system have a more manageable youth unemployment problem than those (such as Britain and France) which do not. In Britain there is considerable dissatisfaction among both employers and school-leavers with the curriculum traditionally followed in most schools, the most frequent criticism being that large parts of it are virtually irrelevant to the needs of industry. Many teachers have had no experience of industry themselves and, as a result, are in no position to give their pupils any useful advice about jobs.[11] Until these glaring weaknesses in the education system itself are corrected, the Manpower Services Commission can do little more than tinker with the problem of youth unemployment. Industry itself must also share some of the blame in so far as three-fifths of the young people who enter employment for the first time each year go into jobs where they receive practically no training. Consequently their work experience does little to enhance their future employment prospects.

Faced with these fundamental problems the Commission has hitherto been obliged to confine itself to providing an 'ambulance service' for those young people who find themselves out of work. Initially the main emphasis was on creating jobs for young people and offering recruitment subsidies to employers. Since 1977, however, the provision of training facilities has become more important and these are now offered under the umbrella of the Youth Opportunities Programme. The programme offers a range of opportunities in vocational preparation courses and work experience, structured in 'modules' so that the needs of individuals can be met. The courses are necessarily of short duration so that the maximum annual throughput of people in the 16–18 age group can be achieved.[12] It would be naive to suppose, however, that courses of this kind can make up for the time which young people may have wasted either at school or in their first job. It would be equally naive to assume that a few months' 'work experience' will in itself transform the longer-term employment prospects of those involved. The success of this part of the YOP depends on the willingness of employers to provide jobs which are likely to have some experiential value for young people, and so far the response from industry has been less than enthusiastic. We must not lose sight of the fact that the Youth Opportunities Programme can at most only ease the mismatch problem by increasing the supply of young people who are equipped for work. It will increase the *demand* for young people only to the extent that it overcomes the prejudice which many employers are said to harbour against them.

But employer hostility is itself only one element in the problem of youth unemployment, and a policy designed to remove mismatches should also seek to encourage labour mobility. The term 'mobility' is normally used to describe the movement of workers out of declining industries into those with a future both within and between localities and regions. During the Second World War a large number of workers transferred their employment from one area to another with the assistance of the government, but in the post-war period this kind of mobility rapidly disappeared, while the conventional wisdom behind the regional policies which were formulated in the 1960s was that jobs should be moved to people. Large employers were given generous financial incentives to set up plants in the 'depressed' regions, though the effects of this policy on regional *employment* growth seem to have been considerably less significant than was initially anticipated.[13] During the 1960s only about 1,000 workers a year were receiving financial assistance from the government in moving from one job to another. In 1972 the employment transfer scheme was re-vamped in response to rising unemployment and the following year over 17,000 people took advantage of it, but since then, numbers have fallen off very sharply.

In its 1977 report the MSC made financial provision for 22,000 assisted moves but this seems very optimistic. Up to 1974 nearly one-third of assisted migrant workers were from Scotland; thereafter the North Sea oil industry has generated a rapid expansion of job opportunities within Scotland, reducing the incentive for unemployed Scots to move south.[14] It has also been reported that relatively few unemployed or redundant workers in any region actually know about the employment transfer scheme.[15] The scheme itself has certain technical weaknesses. Grants are given to assist workers with house purchase, removal and legal expenses are paid, and disturbance allowances are also available. But accommodation still seems to be a disincentive, especially among those workers who are looking for council houses. Many local authorities impose a two-year residence qualification on 'immigrants' before any applications for council houses can even be considered. It is hardly surprising, therefore, that a large minority of workers who have used the transfer scheme return home within a year. The fundamental reason for the low take-up rate of financial assistance, however, is that in a severe recession the vast majority of the unemployed prefer to be unemployed in their own communities rather than go to all the trouble of moving somewhere else where the chances of further unemployment may be quite high. It was pointed out in Chapter Three that regional disparities in unemployment rates have narrowed in recent years and that no region has escaped the trends affecting the country as a whole, so the reluctance of the unemployed to look for work elsewhere has a degree of rationality.

A labour market strategy which aims primarily to remove mismatches, promote mobility and thus reduce the natural rate of unemployment does not depend for its success on an increase in the total number of jobs in the economy. It simply seeks to create a better match, both occupationally and geographically, between vacancies and the unemployed and relies predominantly on training programmes to achieve this objective. The foregoing discussion, however, suggests that since the most important mismatches are the result of several different factors, social as well as economic, they are unlikely to be removed by training alone. It follows that the strategy currently being pursued by the MSC in this field is unlikely to have more than a marginal impact on the aggregate unemployment figures, at least in the short term. In these circumstances it is hardly surprising that governments should have turned to more direct forms of intervention which, while doing little to correct the structural weaknesses of the labour market, may have some effect on the level of demand for labour and thus reduce the total volume of unemployment.

Creating and subsidizing employment

It was argued above that the Youth Opportunities Programme can do no more than tackle the symptoms of a problem whose roots lie partly within the education system and partly within industry itself. Since 1975, however, policy-makers have been forced to come to terms with the reality of an ever-increasing number of unskilled, unqualified and untrained young people who enter the labour market and fail to find work. The longer-term social consequences of youth unemployment can hardly be ignored: 'Give a young person six months of feeling worthless and you might have a lifetime delinquent, permanently unemployed and perhaps unemployable.'[16] At an early stage of the recent recession it was recognized, therefore, that jobs would have to be created in order to keep the least employable members of the young workforce off the streets. In essence the Job Creation Programme (renamed the Special Temporary Employment Programme in 1977) was conceived as an extension of the State-financed public works programmes which countries such as Canada have long been operating.

The first objective of the JCP was to provide work for people (especially those in the 16–25 age group) who would otherwise be unemployed. Between October 1975 and September 1977 approximately 90,000 jobs were created under the programme, the principal beneficiaries being the least qualified members of the unemployed labour force under the age of 25.[17] This figure is, however, misleading because the average length of projects approved under the JCP was little more than six months. At any one time, the number of people employed on JCP projects was likely to be considerably smaller than the overall figure implies. In August 1977, for example, only 42,500 people were employed on JCP projects. In all probability many of these would have returned to the unemployment register once their project had been completed.

The second objective of the JCP was to provide work which

was of value both to the community as a whole and to the individual. But in setting themselves this task the organizers faced a dilemma, as one observer pointed out at the start of the JCP:

On the one hand they want to encourage labour-intensive schemes to provide as much work as possible for the unemployed. Environmental jobs like clearing derelict sites and turning them into golf courses or adventure playgrounds have been mentioned as suitable candidates. At the same time the organizers don't want to create 'dead-end jobs' but work with a training potential. What kind of skills can be provided on short-term jobs – other than basic induction into the work situation – remains unclear. And the more the numbers on the programme, the less chance of training.[18]

This dilemma has not yet been resolved and some of the projects which were devised in the early days of the JCP (such as cleaning up beaches) attracted much adverse publicity. Nevertheless, as the organizers have gained more experience so the educational value of JCP work seems to have risen. It will always, of course, be vulnerable to the charge of being a short-term cosmetic. It is also fair to point out that most of the projects have been provided by local authorities for the simple reason that the JCP offers a convenient method of financing environmental work which would not otherwise be undertaken due to the severe restraints on local government spending. But as long as the JCP makes some contribution, however modest, to the task of preventing a large number of young people from becoming virtually unemployable, it should be retained and if possible gradually extended.

The JCP is, however, only one aspect of a much wider programme of subsidizing employment. In August 1975 the government introduced the Temporary Employment Subsidy (TES) which is designed to maintain employment in firms where redundancies would otherwise take place. The scheme provides employers with a subsidy of £20 per week for each job they agree to maintain. It is paid only as long as the job remains at risk and for a maximum period of one year, although if the job is still at risk at the end of this period a further subsidy of £10 per week is available for six months. Insolvent firms, or those near to insolvency, are not eligible for TES. Not surprisingly, the response from industry has been favourable. By March 1978 a total of 408,000 jobs had attracted the £20 subsidy, and a further 66,000 jobs had been given the £10 supplementary subsidy. In February 1978 the government announced plans to extend the subsidy scheme to the *recruitment* of workers, thereby imitating the West German approach to subsidizing employment. It would seem that the concept is here to stay, unless of course a change of government brings a more hostile approach.

The case for employment subsidies as a vital part of a strategy against unemployment is undoubtedly persuasive. It was pointed out in Chapter Four that Keynesians and monetarists alike have emphasized the importance of reducing the real supply cost of labour if employment is to be stimulated. If, however, this involves a sustained reduction in real wages, trade union opposition will be encountered. Employment subsidies reconcile these conflicting pressures by cutting the cost of hiring labour while simultaneously preserving real incomes. Subsidies also entail a low or even zero net cost in public expenditure because a worker who is kept in his job, or one who is taken off the unemployment register and put into a job, does not claim any of the transfer payments to the unemployed. He also goes on contributing to aggregate output and consumption and thereby helps to avoid a downward spiral into depression. By enabling firms to maintain a relatively high level of capacity-utilization, employment subsidies can contribute to lower unit costs and thus help firms to survive a recession. One might also add that practically every other Western European country uses employment subsidies in one form or another and that it would be absurd for British employers to be denied the assistance which their continental competitors enjoy.

Employment subsidies are, however, open to criticism. Firstly it has been argued that job-preserving and recruitment subsidies can only save or create jobs at someone else's expense: 'Such subsidies reduce the relative costs and prices of the firms receiving them and thereby cause a substitution of consumer expenditure away from the products of non-subsidized firms whose output and employment will be reduced.'[19] While theoretically valid, this argument needs to be seen in the context of Britain's balance of payments constraint. It has been reported that nearly half of all TES workers are in the textiles, clothing and footwear industries, all of which have been severely affected by the sharp rise in cheap imports from the newly industrializing countries. If, therefore, TES has had any damaging effects on employment, these will largely have been felt abroad. Secondly, it is argued that TES is far too indiscriminate in so far as it falls like 'God's gentle rain' on firms which are experiencing a temporary shortage of business and on those which are in long-term decline. Those who believe that the British textiles and clothing industries have no future and that their existing manpower must therefore be released and re-deployed as soon as possible may well regard TES as an expensive short-term cosmetic which is likely to make the process of long-term structural change even more difficult than it would other-wise be. Yet the available evidence would hardly justify such a sweeping condemnation. A survey by the Department of Employment in 1978 of measures taken by firms *after* the cessation of TES payments revealed that one-third had been able to withdraw from the scheme before the twelve-month time limit had expired (mainly because of an upturn in business) and that a further one-third had taken on additional labour. The survey found that only 12 per cent of TES workers were declared redundant after the payments ceased.[20] This suggests that the majority of firms who received TES were in a stronger position after the subsidy ended than they were at the outset.

A more powerful objection is that a job-preserving subsidy such as TES simply encourages employers to retain labour which really ought to be 'shaken out'. At the same time it relieves the pressure on employers and unions to find other ways of increasing job security (for example through higher productivity) and merely adds to the general problems of overmanning and inefficiency. For this reason, some commentators have urged the government to abandon job-preservation and instead to subsidize the recruit-ment of workers, as indeed every other EEC country does to a greater or lesser degree.[21] In fact the Labour government began to adopt this approach in 1976 with the introduction of a Youth Employment Subsidy. Under this scheme employers were encouraged to recruit young people aged under 20 who had been continuously unemployed for six months or more. For each eligible young person recruited for full-time work, employers were paid £10 a week for up to six months. Between October 1976 and February 1978 (when the scheme was absorbed into the Manpower Services Commission's Youth Opportunities Programme), a total 38,500 young workers were covered by the subsidy. The effect of the subsidy on the actual level of recruitment, however, seems to have been modest. A survey by the Department of Employment suggests that about 75 per cent of the subsidized young people would have been recruited regardless of the subsidy. The larger the firm, the less impact the subsidy seemed to have.[22]

The response to the Small Firms Employment Subsidy (SFES), introduced in July 1977, was more positive. From July 1977 until March 1978 small firms in the Special Development Areas of the North East, North West, Wales and Scotland were able to claim £20 a week for each full-time job and £10 for every part-time job which they provided. These payments were made for up to 26 weeks for each extra job. The obvious objection to any form of recruitment subsidy is that most of the money would go to those firms who already intended to expand, but the results of the SFES experiment (which is, apparently, to be re-introduced on a large scale) suggest that this criticism is only partly valid. A limited survey of SFES firms on Merseyside suggests that about half the jobs would have been created when they were, regardless of the subsidy. Of those jobs which were actually created by the subsidy, it was anticipated that about 66 per cent would outlast its termination. This suggests that the subsidy was not only regarded as a method of reducing wage costs but might in addition have encouraged some employers to reduce overtime and negotiate new working practices.[23]

The main effect of all employment subsidies must, however, fall on the real supply cost of labour. Orthodox economic theory implies that, by reducing this cost, subsidies should positively encourage employment as well as prevent a further rise in unemployment. The evidence quoted above suggests that in certain instances this may well be true. The main weakness of subsidies is that they may simply prolong the life of low-paid, low-productivity industries and thus inhibit the longer-term processes of structural change. In Britain, however, the main impact of these subsidies has been concentrated in those industries which are most vulnerable to imports from newly industrializing countries where labour costs are extremely low. They may therefore be seen as consistent with the policy of direct import controls which has already been applied in these industries. In other industries job-preserving subsidies can be justified as long as they are used to tide firms over a temporary contraction in demand. If they did not exist, these firms would have no option but to declare redundancies, and as long as the retraining of redundant workers continues to be a low priority this outcome must surely be avoided wherever possible. A job-preserving subsidy can provide both employers and workers with a breathing space during which the longer-term pressures facing the firm can be assessed and measures taken to improve efficiency which do not necessarily involve compulsory redundancy. A recruitment subsidy can create a certain amount of employment, or at least bring forward recruitment decisions, and may be marginally useful in encouraging employers to hire more young people. The effectiveness of this policy will, however, be reduced if other elements in the real supply cost of labour (for example the employer's national insurance contributions) are rising, as they were in Britain during 1976–8.

Work-sharing

Even the most enthusiastic advocates of subsidizing and creating jobs would admit that these measures can at best have only a marginal effect on the demand for labour. A vigorous expansion of demand by conventional Keynesian methods is, however, rejected by almost every Western government for fear of provoking higher inflation and/or a balance of payments deficit. In these circumstances governments have been forced to consider the idea of sharing the available work out among more people by reducing the average number of hours worked by those in employment. Work-sharing may in theory be achieved by reducing the basic weekly hours of work, reducing overtime working, increasing annual holiday entitlements and encouraging older workers to retire early. It has certain attractions in Britain where average weekly hours are higher and basic holiday entitlements lower than in most other Western countries, but it does raise a number of problems.

A reduction in basic weekly hours of work has been advocated on social as well as economic grounds. Hughes, for example, has pointed out that in Britain only about 11 per cent of male manual full-time workers have a basic week of 38 hours or less, whereas the coresponding proportion in the non-manual grades is 75 per cent. Consequently a reduction in the basic working week from 40 to 37 hours would create most employment for male manual workers who, of course, are disproportionately affected by unemployment.[24] It is by no means certain, however, that reducing normal hours would in practice bring a corresponding fall in unemployment. In the past such reductions have been partly offset by an increase in overtime working, and since male manual workers are responsible for 80 per cent of all overtime hours it is likely that the same might happen again. A further difficulty is that employers may not be able to group the 'lost' hours into full-time job units. Some of this 'loss' might thus become permanent – especially if a firm already had spare capacity – and there would be a corresponding rise in output per man hour. Estimates of the job-creating effects of a shorter working week depend, therefore, on varying assumptions about changes in overtime and productivity. The Department of Employment has calculated that if normal weekly hours were cut to 35, the fall in registered unemployment could be 'anywhere between 100,000 and 500,000'. But if weekly earnings were maintained, a reduction of this magnitude could increase total labour costs by between 6 and 8 per cent with predictable effects on industrial competitiveness.[25]

One alternative to reducing the basic week would be to bring down the level of overtime working. In 1976–7 a total of 16·5 million hours of overtime were worked in British industry; in the manufacturing sector about a third of the labour force regularly work over 8 hours overtime per week. If all the overtime worked in manufacturing industry could be parcelled into full-time job units, this would immediately absorb all the registered unemployed in this sector. A more modest reduction might still have significant effects. Thus the Department of Employment has suggested that if *half* of all hours at present worked by manual men in excess of 48 per week were instead worked by additional full-time workers, the number of registered unemployed could be cut by 100,000.[26]

During 1978 the TUC responded by launching a drive to restrict overtime to the equivalent of 5 hours a week which, if successful, would certainly make an impact on unemployment. In practice such well-meaning initiatives are unlikely to have much effect. Many employers would argue that overtime can be an efficient way of increasing output and that in any case most of the 'lost' overtime hours could not be grouped into full-time job units. Trade unionists in the low wage industries would point out that regular overtime is an essential element in their weekly earnings without which they could not maintain a tolerable standard of living. Any attempt to reduce overtime by law would therefore fall hardest on low-paid workers and would no doubt be strenuously resisted by their organizations. The only alternative method would be to encourage employers and trade unionists to negotiate changes in working practices and pay structures which reduced the need for overtime. This approach was in fact adopted during the 1960s when productivity bargaining was in vogue. The results, however, suggest that workers will make concessions on overtime only if their basic pay is increased by the appropriate amount. One suspects that in practice very few workers would be prepared to stand a permanent loss in their overtime pay simply in order to provide work for the unemployed.

An increase in annual holiday entitlements would have a similarly modest impact on unemployment. Britain is the only EEC country which does not lay down a minimum holiday entitlement by law, but the gap between Britain and the rest of the EEC is not at present very great. In 1975 the EEC recommended that member states should move towards four weeks' paid annual holiday for all workers and Britain is now quite close to this level. Any further increase in basic holidays would not have much effect on unemployment as the 'lost' time would almost certainly be absorbed in increased overtime or higher productivity. Trade unions might also insist that employers should begin to follow the example of their counterparts in Belgium, France and West Germany and give generous holiday bonuses.[27] To the extent that they were successful, wage costs would be increased and the pressure to find offsetting gains in productivity would be all the greater.

In summary, the case in favour of work-sharing as a remedy for unemployment is only superficially attractive. If either basic weekly hours or overtime hours were reduced and holiday entitlements increased, then in theory the employed workforce would have more leisure time at its disposal (which would in turn increase employment in leisure services) and thousands of jobs would be created for the unemployed. In practice these benefits are unlikely to be realized. Increased leisure time, if it is to be enjoyed, requires an appropriate level of real income which in turn depends on productivity. In the rest of the EEC, employers and trade unions have pursued a deliberate strategy of reducing working hours, without loss of earnings, through productivity improvements. Such a strategy would be extremely relevant to Britain's present economic problems but it would hardly create more employment. There is a great deal of evidence to suggest that in British industry a large proportion of the normal working week is being used unproductively. A low average level of efficiency obviously has several causes, but the importance of poor managerial organization has been emphasized by many researchers.[28] A reduction in the basic working week to, say, 35 hours and an addition of one week to the present annual holiday entitlement of manual workers could therefore be justified on the grounds that with less time at their disposal, employers would either have to find more efficient methods of getting work done or face damaging increases in unit costs. The results in terms of job creation would, however, be extremely modest.

As an alternative to manipulating hours of work, governments can take direct action to reduce the labour supply. One much-canvassed example of such action would be to reduce the retiring age for men to 60. The Department of Employment has estimated that this would immediately take 200,000 people off the unemployment register, a figure which would probably swell to 600,000 once industry had adjusted itself to the change. Set against this obvious benefit is the cost of implementing the scheme. The extra pension payments and lost income-tax revenue would cost between £1·8 and £2·5 billion a year, but this would have to be offset against the reduction in transfer payments to the unemployed, leaving a net cost to the government of £1 billion a year.[29] In fact this seems a relatively small price to pay for such a major reduction in unemployment when it is remembered that in 1976–7 alone the government lost an estimated £1·2 billion in tax and national insurance revenues and paid a total of £1·4 billion in various benefits to the unemployed.[30]

A more philosophical objection to reducing the age of compulsory retirement is based on the belief that it is both morally wrong and economically wasteful to force large numbers of people who may be physically and mentally capable of working into premature idleness. Without entering into this debate, we may simply make two observations. Firstly, the present retirement age for men was introduced in 1925 in response to the argument that lowering the pensionable age (from 70, where it had been since 1908) would release jobs for the younger unemployed.[31] There is, in other words, nothing sacrosanct about the age limit of 65. Secondly, there has in recent years been a general tendency for occupational and company pension schemes to provide for retirement at 60 or earlier. In 1977, for example, the National Union of Mineworkers negotiated an agreement with the National Coal Board whereby miners may retire at 62 on a retirement pension equal to 85 per cent of take-home pay based on average earnings. Most public sector agreements do not *compel* men to retire at the 'normal' age and in practice the 'average' retirement age may be anything up to four years beyond it.[32] It is always possible that some employers may take advantage of early retirement in order to reduce their manpower requirements. But even so the impact on the unemployment figures would still be substantially greater than any of the alternative schemes discussed above.

By contrast, the government's Job Release Scheme (JRS) has been a failure. When the JRS was introduced in January 1977, it offered workers who were within one year of the national insurance pension age a tax-free allowance if they agreed to withdraw prematurely from the labour market. Initially it was restricted to the Assisted Areas but in March 1978 it was extended to the whole country. It is a condition of the scheme that the employer agrees to recruit someone from the unemployment register when a JRS applicant leaves his job. The scheme is, however, entirely voluntary and its success must therefore depend on the financial incentive it gives to early retirement. In fact, between July 1977 and March 1978 less than 7,000 JRS applications were made, the main reason being that the tax-free allowance (of £23 a week, rising to £26·50 in November 1977) was considered inadequate by many of those who were eligible to apply.[33] In Belgium job release is open to any worker within *five* years of retirement and the weekly allowance payable under the scheme is reported to be between 75 and 85 per cent of the individual worker's previous net wage.[34] A similar approach would be well worth trying in Britain since it *could* have a significant impact on the unemployment figures while avoiding the compulsion inherent in a reduction of the national insurance retirement age.

The future course of labour market policy

Within a few years labour market policy in Britain has been transformed. Up to 1973 the dominant philosophy was still one of benign neglect. The role of the State extended no further than the provision of limited financial incentives which, it was hoped, would induce employers to train more workers and persuade workers themselves to accept displacement and mobility. While this approach could be justified in a market environment characterized by net excess demand for labour, it has become increasingly inappropriate in a period of relatively high and rising unemployment. Since 1975 various expedients have been adopted which, in total, represent the abandonment of the traditional approach. Some of these have been introduced primarily in order to effect a short-term reduction in the aggregate unemployment figures; others have been designed with a view to alleviating the more conspicuous mismatches in the labour market. Most, however, look as though they could easily become permanent features of labour market policy. The question which must be answered is whether these various measures add up to a coherent strategy designed to reduce unemployment in the longer-term and, if not, what further action needs to be taken.

Our previous analysis of Britain's unemployment problem suggests that the structural mismatches in the labour market have grown worse in recent years. For any given level of registered unemployment there are more vacancies than there used to be, while the shortfall in the supply of certain types of skilled manpower has increased. If it is assumed that manufacturing industry will continue to shed labour over the next decade, then the problem of retraining older workers will become increasingly acute. The obvious response to these pressures would be to expand the provision of training facilities at skill centres far beyond the 22,000 places which are supposed to be available by 1981. A comprehensive training strategy must seek both to equip more school-leavers and young workers generally with marketable skills and to provide older, experienced workers with more opportunities to acquire new skills. The current level of provision in both these areas is manifestly inadequate in relation to the demands which the manpower service agencies are likely to encounter during the 1980s. Training alone, however, will not be enough to correct these mismatches. If the overall supply of skilled men is to be brought into line with the changing needs of the economy, there will have to be a radical improvement in the pay, status and security of these groups. This objective will in turn have far-reaching implications for the development of incomes policy at national level and for the management of industrial relations in the workplace.

The government will also have to develop a comprehensive *mobility* policy to help workers move between areas and between occupations. Two problems must be overcome in this field before such a policy could emerge. Firstly, the various financial inducements on offer only become effective *after* a move has taken place and do not therefore exert much influence over the decision to move.[35] Secondly, the housing policy of most local authorities does not encourage geographical mobility. The reasons are quite understandable, but it is difficult to envisage any solution to this problem which does not involve the conversion of a large section of the public housing stock to owner occupation.[36]

To the extent that this strategy succeeded in improving the supply of labour relative to demand it would have an appreciable effect on the natural rate of unemployment. It could be argued, however, that policies which are designed to inflate the short-term demand for labour irrespective of the structural weaknesses in the market may well tend to *increase* the natural rate. A job-creation programme which largely provides temporary spells of unskilled work for unskilled young people can contribute little, if anything, to the task of improving the employability of this group. Similarly, a job-preservation subsidy which simply keeps people in uneconomic jobs and declining industries can, by weakening or postponing the impact of structural change and foreign competition, encourage both workers and employers to retain inefficient practices. The problem is that if neither job creation nor job preservation had been grafted on to government policy, the aggregate level of unemployment would be considerably higher than it is. Until our approach to redundancy and retraining is brought into line with contemporary circumstances, it is difficult to argue that employment subsidies should be discarded. In any case they can always be justified for those firms which have encountered a temporary contraction in business and simply need something to help them avoid unnecessary redundancies. Likewise job-creation schemes, with all their faults, are by no means irrelevant to the problem of dealing with some of the least employable entrants into the labour market. It is very difficult in practice for many of those employed on job-creation schemes to find more constructive forms of employment, or take some kind of further education or training course. In their case the choice is usually between temporary employment and permanent idleness. Consequently it is difficult to see how job creation and job subsidies can be abandoned as long as other policies remain unchanged.

The adoption of a comprehensive work-sharing strategy (which at the time of writing has not happened in Britain) might also help to raise the natural unemployment rate in the long term *if* the anticipated short-term effects on the level of employment were actually realized. If either the basic working week or the average level of overtime were reduced and the 'lost' hours were successfully parcelled up into 'job units', labour costs would undoubtedly rise more sharply than otherwise and the immediate gain in employment might soon be cancelled out. The main impact of a shorter working week is likely to be on productivity rather than employment, however, and this, indeed, is its principal justification. The only way in which unemployment could be reduced without risking a corresponding fall in productivity would be to fix the statutory retiring age for men at 60 or, alternatively, to develop a much more ambitious and imaginative job-release programme. These measures, along with a reduction in the basic working week and an increase in holiday entitlements, have been criticized on the grounds that they are irreversible and would act as a severe constraint on the labour supply in a period of sustained economic expansion. In reply we might simply note that there seems little possibility in the foreseeable future of securing a rate of economic growth which is likely to create a *general* shortage of labour. Even if the economy defied all expectations and began to move towards fuller employment, the supply constraint might not become serious if employers and trade unions exploited the productivity potential of shorter hours.

Although the need to improve productivity is now widely accepted, there is little agreement on how it should be done. Many trade unionists fear that the pursuit of higher productivity is merely a gateway to widespread redundancy and therefore tend to resist any attempt by managements to increase efficiency if this means a loss of jobs. If all redundant workers had the right to be retrained without significant loss of income during the retraining period, the opposition to redundancy *might* be lessened. The immediate cost of this policy in terms of higher public expenditure would easily be offset by the long-term benefits to the economy as a whole as well as to the workers themselves. The practical difficulty with such a policy is that the government would need to have a very clear picture of the kind of jobs which redundant workers could be trained to do. An agency such as the MSC could only formulate objectives and allocate resources on the basis of reliable information about future trends in the demand for specific kinds of manpower. Such information would have to be provided by a wide range of public and private organizations as well as by individual employers, who would not of course be able to do so unless they had already planned their own manpower requirements.

It is difficult to exaggerate the contribution which effective manpower planning could make towards the success of an active labour market policy. Manpower planning should, at least in theory, help employers to match individuals correctly with appropriate vacancies in the organization, to improve the efficiency with which manpower is used, and to control manpower levels and costs. By forecasting their future labour requirements, managers have more chance of avoiding redundancies and thus of maintaining stability of employment through the economic cycle. As the authors of a recent survey point out, the process of converting sales and production plans into an employment forecast, which in turn forms the basis of a recruitment plan, compels managers to define what they think is an appropriate level of labour productivity for their business.[37] In practice, of course, this is by no means easy to achieve, particularly in the case of those jobs where work measurement techniques are difficult to apply. Nevertheless, the evidence indicates that manpower planning *can* give managers a much greater awareness of trends in the supply of and demand for labour in relation to their business. In Britain this kind of planning has become more widespread in recent years, partly as a result of the general rise in labour costs and partly due to the influence of legislation such as the Equal Pay Act. But there is still much scope for improvement, particularly in respect of forecasting trends in labour supply and training needs, and in involving trade union representatives in the planning process.[38] One possible way of accelerating progress in this field would be for the government to impose a legal requirement on all firms employing, say, more than 500 workers (the limit could subsequently be reduced) to produce a five-year manpower plan for inspection and comment by the MSC. In the case of unionized firms, managements would be required at the very least to consult trade union representatives before submitting their plan. While the reliability of these plans would no doubt vary with the expertise of the managers who drew them up, the MSC would at least have much more information about anticipated trends in supply and demand than it has at the moment. To this extent its own plans for expanding its training and re-training facilities would be more relevant to the needs of industry.

Summary

Writing in the pre-1914 era, Beveridge defined Britain's unemployment problem as follows:

> The problem is essentially one of business organization, of meeting without distress the changes and fluctuations without which industry is not and probably could not be carried on. It is not a problem of increasing the mere scale of industry. It is not a problem of securing a general balance between the growth of the demand for labour and the growth of the supply – for this general balance is already secured by economic forces – but one of perfecting the adjustment in detail ... The paradox has to be faced – that the creation or provision of work is the one thing that is no remedy for unemployment. It may palliate immediate distress. It may increase general prosperity. It may cause unemployment for a while to be forgotten. It does not banish disorganization from the State.[39]

Our confidence in the benign working of 'economic forces' cannot be equal to that of Beveridge, and the role of demand factors must never be overlooked. Nevertheless, Beveridge's analysis underlines the dilemma which currently confronts public policy-makers. On the one hand they have an understandable wish to be seen to be 'doing something' about unemployment. On the other hand, it is generally recognized that some of the measures which can in the short term reduce unemployment may actually aggravate the problem in the longer term.

A logical case can be argued in favour of a strategy whose main purpose is to *protect* employment. Such a strategy would include stringent controls on imports, generous subsidies to firms and industries which were in danger of collapse, and measures to promote work-sharing. The problem is that by protecting the *status quo* in employment terms this strategy would also in effect

129

be helping to preserve thousands of low-paid jobs with low productivity. It is not immediately obvious that protectionism – in its widest sense – would encourage managers and trade unionists to get to grips with the problem of low productivity. On the other hand it must also be recognized that if the government were to withdraw all employment subsidies, the cost to the public purse in terms of higher unemployment would be enormous. In the long run, the only strategy which will succeed in preventing unemployment from reaching the levels which some economists have predicted is one which encourages the market sector of the economy to *generate more* employment. Temporary subsidies can be justified if, as seems to be the case, they help firms to overcome short-term fluctuations in demand. The logic of providing huge, open-ended subsidies to inefficient, uncompetitive firms simply because they are large employers of labour must, however, be questioned.

If the market sector of the economy is to be strengthened, the balance of payments constraint on growth must be removed. This will require a sustained increase in the average level of productivity in British manufacturing industry. It is in this context that the role of incomes policy should be seen. Higher productivity is an objective to which the reform of collective bargaining at plant and national level could make an important contribution. Incomes policy has been used in the past as a means of encouraging employers and trade unionists to negotiate about more efficient working practices and could be so used again. But it would also have to be accompanied by a new approach to redundancy as well as a more liberal attitude towards profit and enterprise. If investment in the growth sectors of the economy is to be increased, governments will have to recognize that the average return to the investor must be greatly improved. But this in turn presupposes the existence of a climate of opinion which is much more favourable towards effort and reward than at present, and the political difficulties which stand in the way of such a change can hardly be exaggerated. The further development of tripartite policy-making at national level, reinforced by the growth of worker participation in management at company level, would no doubt be relevant to this objective. But no one should be under any illusions about the difficulty of changing traditional attitudes. In this sense it could be said that in so far as there *is* a solution to our unemployment problem, it depends more on the political will of governments, employers and trade unionists than on the prescriptions of economists.

Notes

Chapter Two
Does Britain Have an Unemployment Problem?

1. W. H. Beveridge, *Unemployment: A Problem of Industry*, Longmans, 1909, p. 111.

2. ibid., p. 220.

3. Derek Aldcroft and Peter Fearon (Eds.), *Economic Growth in Twentieth Century Britain*, Macmillan, 1969, p. xxx.

4. Sidney Pollard, *The Development of the British Economy 1914–1950*, Edward Arnold, 1962, p. 247.

5. ibid., p. 248.

6. Milton Friedman, *Unemployment versus Inflation?*, (Occasional Paper No. 44), Institute of Economic Affairs, 1975, p. 17.

7. B. Corry and D. Laidler, 'The Phillips Curve: A Theoretical Explanation', *Economica*, Vol. XX, 1967.

8. 'The Unemployment Statistics and their Interpretation', *Department of Employment Gazette*, March 1975.

9. These figures are, of course, only estimates by the Department. No conclusive evidence is available because the monthly count does not refer to *completed* spells of employment. See *Department of Employment Gazette*, February 1973 and June 1978.

10. 'New Projections of Future Labour Force', *Department of Employment Gazette*, June 1977.

11. John B. Wood, *How Little Unemployment?*, (Hobart Paper No. 65), Institute of Economic Affairs, 1975, pp. 23–4.

12. *Department of Employment Gazette*, February 1978. The proportion was almost exactly the same for both men and women. In January 1976, by contrast, some 22 per cent of men in this age group had been unemployed for more than 6 months, whereas among women the proportion was only 16 per cent – *Department of Employment Gazette*, 1976.

13. John B. Wood, *How Much Unemployment?*, (Research Monograph No. 28), Institute of Economic Affairs, 1972, p. 16.

14. D. I. Mackay, 'After the Shake-Out', *Oxford Economic Papers*, Vol. 24, March 1972.

15. James J. Hughes, 'How should we measure unemployment?', *British Journal of Industrial Relations*, Vol. 13, November 1975.

16. ibid.

17. Wood, op. cit., pp. 30–31.

18. 'The Unemployment Statistics and their Interpretation', *Department of Employment Gazette*, March 1975.

19. 'Characteristics of the Unemployed', *Department of Employment Gazette*, June 1977.

20. In June 1973 the D of E asked its staff in the employment offices to make subjective judgements on the prospects and attitudes to work of a large sample of adults on the register. The survey showed that 40 per cent of men were judged to have good prospects of finding long-term work and were keen to do so; 30 per cent were keen but had poor prospects; 30 per cent were not enthusiastic and had poor prospects. A follow-up survey in January 1974 found that two-thirds of those reckoned to have good prospects in June 1973 had found work, while one-third of those with poor prospects had also got jobs – *Department of Employment Gazette*, March 1975.

21. Hughes, op. cit.

22. Frank Field (Ed.), *The Conscript Army: A Study of Britain's Unemployed*, Routledge, 1977, pp. 7–8.

23. Wood, op. cit., pp. 25–7.

24. J. Bourlet and A. Bell, *Unemployment and Inflation*, Economic Research Council, 1973, p. 14.

25. *Report of the Committee on Abuse of Social Security Benefits*, HMSO, 1973.

26. Hughes, op. cit.

27. Ralph Harris and Brendon Sewill, *British Economic Policy, 1970–1974: Two Views*, Institute of Economic Affairs, 1975, p. 14.

28. *Department of Employment Gazette*, October 1976.

29. W. W. Daniel, *A National Survey of the Unemployed* (Broadsheet No. 546), PEP, October 1974, pp. 151–2.

30. Office of Population, Censuses and Surveys, *Effects of the Redundancy Payments Act*, HMSO, 1971.

31. D. I. Mackay and G. L. Reid, 'Redundancy, Unemployment and Manpower Policies', *Economic Journal*, Vol. 82, December 1972.

32. Alan Evans, 'Notes on the Changing Relationship between Registered Unemployment and Notified Vacancies: 1961–1966 and 1966–1971', *Economica*, Vol. 44, 1977.

33. Dennis Maki and Z. A. Spindler, 'The Effect of Unemployment Compensation on the Rate of Unemployment in Great Britain', *Oxford Economic Papers*, Vol. 27, 1975.

34. 'The Changed Relationship between Unemployment and Vacancies', *Department of Employment Gazette*, October 1976. A

departmental working party concluded that the effect of ERS on male unemployment 'was probably less than 50,000 and was no more than a small part of the shift in the relationship between unemployment and vacancies'.

35. Samuel Brittan, 'Full Employment Policy: A Reappraisal', in G. D. N. Worswick (Ed.), *The Concept and Measurement of Involuntary Unemployment*, Allen and Unwin, 1976, p. 255.

36. NIESR, *National Institute Economic Review*, February 1977, p. 15.

37. W. W. Daniel, 'Is Youth Unemployment Really the Problem?', *New Society*, 10 November 1977.

38. Daniel, 1974, op. cit., pp. 151–2.

39. In Daniel's survey, 72 per cent mentioned 'lack of money', 28 per cent 'boredom and inactivity', 14 per cent 'depression and apathy', and 11 per cent felt themselves to be 'failures' – 1974, op. cit., pp. 42–51.

40. John Hill, 'The Psychological Impact of Unemployment', *New Society*, 19 January 1978.

Chapter Three

Particular People, Particular Places

1. A survey by the National Child Development Study in 1974 found that half of all 16-year-olds wanted to leave school in order to earn a wage and be independent as soon as possible; a fifth said they did not like school work, and a fifth felt they were not good enough to stay on – *Social Trends*, HMSO, 1977.

2. *Review and Plan, 1977*, Manpower Services Commission.

3. J. L. Baxter, 'Long-Term Unemployment in Britain, 1953–1971', *Bulletin of the Oxford Institute of Economics and Statistics*, Vol. 34, 1972.

4. *Department of Employment Gazette*, June 1977.

5. *The Economist*, 11 June 1977.

6. 'The Young and Out of Work', *Department of Employment Gazette*, August 1978.

7. ibid.

8. This adult-youth wage differential has in fact been steadily declining since the 1950s, but the rise since 1971 has been exceptionally sharp – ibid.

9. Reported in *Department of Employment Gazette*, December 1977. These complaints are not peculiar to British employers. A French employment-service official, for example, was quoted in a *Sunday Times*

survey of youth unemployment in Europe (15 June 1975) as saying: 'What do you expect when the education system turns out youngsters totally untrained for a job or even for life itself? They demand well-paid work as soon as they leave school. What we need are youngsters conditioned to the hardships of life and the grim existence of the factory floor.'

10. *New Society*, 5 February 1976.

11. 'Young People Leaving School', *Department of Employment Gazette*, June 1978.

12. ibid.

13. W. W. Daniel and Elizabeth Stilgoe, 'Towards an American Way of Unemployment?', *New Society*, 12 February 1976.

14. W. H. Beveridge, *Unemployment: A Problem of Industry*, Longman, 1908, pp. 120–21.

15. W. W. Daniel, *A National Survey of the Unemployed*, PEP, 1974, pp. 109–10.

16. ibid.

17. In its survey of the characteristics of the unemployed in June 1976, the Department of Employment found that while the over-55 group's prospects of getting work were generally low and fell even further as duration of unemployment increased, their motivation to work remained high – *Department of Employment Gazette*, June 1977.

18. In a recent survey on the impact of employment protection legislation on industrial practices, Daniel found that natural wastage and redeployment were far more common as responses to falling demand than compulsory redundancy – see *Department of Employment Gazette*, June 1978.

19. Daniel, op. cit., pp. 53–4. Slightly more than half of the managerial and white-collar workers in his sample had left their last job on retirement terms, compared with less than one-fifth of the semi-skilled and unskilled workers.

20. Beveridge, op. cit., p. 69.

21. The proportion of those in the general labourer category may well be overstated by the official figures. For job-finding purposes a local employment office may decide that a wider range of unskilled jobs might be suitable for an unemployed man and they may therefore classify him as seeking a 'general labouring' job. Thus the general labourer category in the unemployment statistics contains a relatively high proportion of labourers compared with the number of general labourers in employment – see *Department of Employment Gazette*, May 1974.

22. *Department of Employment Gazette*, May 1978.

23. *The Economist*, 24 June 1978.

24. Between March 1973 and March 1978, registered male unemployment in the managerial and professional grades rose by 96·7 per cent, compared with a rise in total male unemployment of 75·3 per cent – see *Department of Employment Gazette*, October 1975 and May 1978.

25. In the June 1976 survey of the unemployed, the Department of Employment assessed 38 per cent of men in the managerial and professional group as having 'good or fair' prospects of obtaining long-term employment and a further 38 per cent as having 'reasonable' prospects but with limited local opportunities – *Department of Employment Gazette*, June 1977.

26. Graham Hallett, Peter Randall, E. G. West, *Regional Policy For Ever?* (Readings, No. 11), Institute of Economic Affairs, 1973, pp. 79–82.

27. *Department of Employment Gazette*, June 1977 and June 1974.

28. Derek Morris (Ed.), *The Economic System in the UK*, Oxford University Press, 1977, p. 465.

29. *Sunday Times*, 15 September 1975.

30. City of Bradford Metropolitan Council, *District Trends, 1978*.

31. Rupert Nabarro and Colin Watts, 'Looking for Work in Liverpool', *New Society*, 20 January 1977.

32. R. E. Pahl, *Whose City?*, Penguin, 1975, pp. 175–6.

33. Peter Hall, 'The Inner Cities Dilemma', *New Society*, 3 February 1977.

34. ibid. See also Department of the Environment, *Inner Area Studies: Liverpool, Birmingham and Lambeth*, HMSO, 1977.

35. In July 1976 non-white school-leavers constituted 30 per cent of school-leavers without a job; by January 1977, however, this proportion had increased to 40 per cent. Nationally, unemployment among non-whites in the 16–25 age group rose by 450 per cent between February 1974 and February 1977, compared with an increase of 130 per cent for the working population as a whole – *The Times*, 20 December 1977.

36. In Bradford in 1977 one in every five unemployed people was non-white, although only one in eight of the workforce was non-white. Of the 1,500 non-white people on the unemployment register, over 90 per cent lived in the inner city wards – *District Trends, 1978*.

37. It may well be that the rate of unemployment among non-whites in general is seriously underestimated by the official figures. A Home Office report on unemployment among young non-whites in the London boroughs of Brent and Lewisham in 1974 revealed that 57 per cent of the unemployed had *not* registered at an employment exchange

or careers office – Tom Forester, 'Who, Exactly, are the Unemployed?', *New Society*, 13 January 1977.

38. Sidney Pollard, *The Development of the British Economy, 1914–1950*, Edward Arnold, 1963, p. 246.

39. A survey by the Department of Employment in 1974 found that in all regions except Scotland less than 10 per cent of unemployed men were willing to work anywhere which was beyond daily travelling distance – *Department of Employment Gazette*, June 1974.

Chapter Four

Is Full Employment Possible?

1. OECD, *Towards Full Employment and Price Stability*, 1977, p. 179.

2. Frank Field (Ed.), *The Conscript Army: A Study of Britain's Unemployed*, Routledge, 1977, p. 138.

3. W. H. Beveridge, *Unemployment: A Problem of Industry*, Longmans, 1908. Beveridge observed that in the best years even the 'skilled and organized trades' had an unemployment rate of 2 per cent – p. 69.

4. Sir William Beveridge, *Full Employment in a Free Society*, Allen and Unwin, 1944, p. 128. The 3-per-cent figure was reached by allowing 1 per cent for seasonal unemployment, 1 per cent for 'the change of employment incidental to progress', and 1 per cent for the 'special uncertainties of the export trade'.

5. The 1944 White Paper on full employment policy, for example, assumed an average level of unemployment of about 8 per cent. See T. W. Hutchison, *Economics and Economic Policy in Britain, 1946–1966*, Allen and Unwin, 1968, pp. 26–32.

6. W. A. H. Godley and J. R. Shepherd, 'Long-term Growth and Short-term Policy', *National Institute Economic Review*, August 1964.

7. G. D. N. Worswick (Ed.), *The Concept and Measurement of Involuntary Unemployment*, Allen and Unwin, 1976, p. 281.

8. A. W. Phillips, 'The Relation between Unemployment and the Rate of Change in Money Wages, 1861–1957', *Economica*, Vol. 25, November 1958.

9. F. T. Blackaby, 'The Reform of the Wage Bargaining System', *National Institute Economic Review*, August 1978.

10. OECD, op. cit., p. 108.

11. James A. Trevithick, 'Inflation, the Natural Unemployment Rate and the Theory of Economic Policy', *Scottish Journal of Political Economy*, Vol. 23, February 1976.

12. Milton Friedman, *Unemployment versus Inflation?* (Occasional Paper No. 44), Institute of Economic Affairs, 1975, p. 23.

13. ibid., pp. 44–5.

14. Derek Robinson, 'Differentials and Incomes Policy', *Industrial Relations Journal*, Vol. 4, Spring 1973.

15. Recent empirical work suggests that in Britain changes in unemployment have had 'no discernible effect' on the rate of wage inflation – S. G. B. Henry, M. C. Sawyer and P. Smith, 'Models of Inflation in the United Kingdom: An Evaluation', *National Institute Economic Review*, August 1976.

16. John Flemming, *Catch '76* (Occasional Paper No. 47), Institute of Economic Affairs, 1977.

17. The equilibrium real wage may be calculated by adjusting the index of real earnings to take account of movements in productivity and the terms of trade. The estimates quoted in the text assume that average real earnings were at their equilibrium level in the first quarter of 1973. Thus a 1-per-cent change in the terms of trade requires a 0·3-per-cent change in the real wage as imports represent about 30 per cent of GDP, and a 1-per-cent change in productivity requires a 1-per-cent change in real wages. See Flemming, op. cit.

18. Lord Kahn, 'Thoughts on the Behaviour of Wages and Monetarism', *Lloyds Bank Review*, January 1976.

19. Blackaby, op. cit.

20. W. W. Daniel, *The PEP Survey on Inflation* (Broadsheet No. 553), PEP, July 1975, p. 11.

21. J. A. Trevithick, *Inflation: A Guide to the Crisis in Economics*, Penguin Books, 1977, pp. 100–101.

22. For a more detailed analysis of the relationship between employee aspirations and trade union behaviour since the late 1960s see Kevin Hawkins, *The Management of Industrial Relations*, Penguin Books, 1978, pp. 20–23.

23. D. T. Jones, 'Output, Employment and Labour Productivity in Europe since 1955', *National Institute Economic Review*, November 1976.

24. Royal Commission on the Distribution of Income and Wealth, *The Financing of Quoted Companies in the United Kingdom* (Background Paper No. 1), HMSO, 1976.

25. West Midlands Economic Planning Council, 'Industrial Productivity – Scope for Improvement', *Midlands Tomorrow*, No. 8, 1975.

26. C. F. Pratten and A. G. Atkinson, 'The Use of Manpower in British Manufacturing Industry', *Department of Employment Gazette*, June 1976.

27. R. D. Sleeper, 'SET and the Shake-Out: a Note on the Productivity Effects of the Selective Employment Tax', *Oxford Economic Papers*, Vol. 24, March 1972.

28. Richard Wragg and James Robertson, 'Britain's Industrial Performance Since the War', *Department of Employment Gazette*, May 1978.

29. M. Panic (Ed.), *The U.K. and West German Manufacturing Industry, 1954–1972* (Monograph No. 5), NEDO, 1976.

30. ibid.

31. Robert Bacon and Walter Eltis, *Britain's Economic Problem: Too Few Producers*, Macmillan, 1976, pp. 17–18.

32. A. P. Thirlwall, 'The U.K.'s Economic Problem: A Balance of Payments Constraint?', *National Westminster Bank Quarterly Review*, February 1978.

33. P. Maunder (Ed.), *Case Studies in International Economics*, Heinemann, 1977, p. 72.

34. C. L. Pass and J. R. Sparkes, *Trade and Growth*, Heinemann, 1977, p. 120.

35. *Economist*, 27 May 1978.

36. Recent evidence suggests that there is some relationship between investment and export performance. Those industries which between 1970 and 1976 either improved their export trade 'surplus' (chemicals and electrical engineering) or reduced their import 'deficit' (food, drink and tobacco, and furniture) were those which by and large sustained a relatively high rate of increase in their capital stock – *Economist*, 12 November 1977.

37. *National Institute Economic Review*, February 1977.

38. 'New Projections of Future Labour Force', *Department of Employment Gazette*, June 1977.

39. *Review and Plan, 1977*, Manpower Services Commission.

40. Colin Leicester, 'Keeping the jobless in touch with work', *The Times*, 15 May 1978.

41. *Economic Policy Review No. 4*, Department of Applied Economics, University of Cambridge, 1978.

42. Over the period 1960–73 in almost every Western European country the proportion of the labour force working in agriculture fell by nearly half, from 17 per cent to 9 per cent. In Britain, which has long had a much smaller proportion of its workers in agriculture, the reduction was very marginal, from 4·2 to 3·0 per cent – *New Society*, 19 May 1975.

43. *Economist*, 19 August 1978. It has been estimated that visible and concealed unemployment together may have amounted to nearly 9 per cent of Japan's labour force in 1978.

44. *Economist*, 10 June 1978.

45. *New Society*, 12 January 1978.

46. Leicester, op. cit. See also Forester, 'Destined for the Dole?', *New Society*, 16 March 1978.

47. The CBI survey of industry in October 1973, when registered unemployment was almost exactly 500,000, found that 51 per cent of respondents were short of skilled labour, while 27 per cent reported 'other' labour to be a constraint. These shortages far exceeded those reported in the February 1966 survey when the level of registered unemployment was much lower.

48. *National Institute Economic Review*, February 1977.

49. This point was confirmed by the reports of the thirty-three Sector Working Parties which were set up by the government in 1975 as part of its strategy of industrial regeneration. Most of the SWPs made it clear that even if their ambitious growth targets were achieved, the main thrust would come from a more intensive use of existing manpower and capital and from investment in labour-saving equipment. The job-creation effects would, by contrast, be very modest.

Chapter Five

Some Options for Policy-makers

1. Wynne Godley, 'The Case for Import Controls', *Sunday Times*, 28 March 1976.

2. W. M. Corden and Gerhard Fels, *Public Assistance to Industry*, Macmillan, 1976, p. 218.

3. F. T. Blackaby, 'The Reform of the Wage Bargaining System', *National Institute Economic Review*, August 1978.

4. *Economist*, 1 January 1977.

5. A sample survey of those completing TOPS courses in June/July 1976 showed that 84 per cent of the skillcentre trainees and 67 per cent of those at colleges or other establishments had either obtained jobs or proceeded to further training within 3 to 4 months of completing their courses – Manpower Services Commission.

6. 'The Declining Asset', *Department of Employment Gazette*, April 1977.

7. *Department of Employment Gazette*, June 1977. See also R. F. Elliott, 'Inflation and the Irreversible Erosion of Pay Differentials', *Personnel Management*, December 1977.

8. *Department of Employment Gazette*, April 1977.

9. For a discussion of this problem see Kevin Hawkins, *The Management of Industrial Relations*, Penguin Books, 1978, pp. 96–112.

10. Robert Taylor, 'The Redundancy Raffle', *New Society*, 4 March 1976.

11. Joanna Mack, 'From School to Work', *New Society*, 10 March 1977.

12. In its 1977 report the MSC stated that the work preparation courses in the YOP would provide 3,000 places for 60,000 young people a year; the short courses designed to develop basic industrial skills would provide 3 months' training for 25,000 young people a year; the work experience programme would provide 70,000 places.

13. T. W. Buck and M. H. Atkins, 'The Impact of British Regional Policies on Employment Growth', *Oxford Economic Papers*, Vol. 28, March 1976.

14. Robert Taylor, 'Moving to jobs', *New Society*, 20 November 1975.

15. For a general discussion of the problems of job-seeking see W. W. Daniel, *A National Survey of the Unemployed*, PEP, 1974, pp. 68–87.

16. *The Times*, 17 March 1977.

17. A survey by the Manpower Services Commission in 1976 showed that the majority of JCP employees had left school at the earliest opportunity, and only one-third had *any* educational qualifications. Most of those who had worked prior to their JCP employment had had unskilled jobs – *Department of Employment Gazette*, April 1977.

18. *New Society*, 16 October 1975.

19. John Burton, 'Employment Subsidies – the Case For and Against', *National Westminster Bank Quarterly Review*, February 1977.

20. The heavy concentration of TES payments in the textiles and clothing industries is reflected in the regional distribution of this subsidy. The North West, for example, with 12 per cent of total employees in employment, received 27 per cent of TES payments, 'by far the largest measure' – *Department of Employment Gazette*, May 1978.

21. Robert Taylor, 'EEC job subsidies', *New Society*, 2 February 1978. One significant feature of the Dutch and Belgian recruitment subsidies for young people is that they also encourage employers to *train* those they recruit under the scheme.

22. *Department of Employment Gazette*, April 1978.

23. *Department of Employment Gazette*, May 1978.

24. John Hughes, 'Shiftwork and the Shorter Working Week: Two Ways to Make Jobs', *Personnel Management*, May 1977.

25. *Department of Employment Gazette*, April 1978.

26. ibid.

27. A TUC survey in 1975 showed that in Britain only 15 per cent of workers received even their normal average pay when on holiday. In Belgium, Germany, France and Holland, by contrast, most workers receive holiday bonuses amounting to an extra three to four weeks' average pay – *The Economist*, 1 January 1977.

28. Kevin Hawkins, *The Management of Industrial Relations*, Penguin Books, 1978, pp. 85–7.

29. *Department of Employment Gazette*, March 1978.

30. Frank Field (Ed.), *The Conscript Army: A Study of Britain's Unemployed*, Routledge and Kegan Paul, 1977, p. 84.

31. Pat Thane, 'The Muddled History of Retiring at 60 and 65', *New Society*, 3 August 1978.

32. Tom Forester, 'Retirement Trends', *New Society*, 13 January 1977.

33. *Department of Employment Gazette*, April 1978.

34. *New Society*, 8 December 1977.

35. Derek Palmer and David Gleave, 'Moving to Find Work', *New Society*, 31 August 1978.

36. One suggestion (*Economist*, 15 January 1977) is that all local authorities should operate schemes for converting most council house tenancies into council mortgages, thus giving the occupiers both the right to sell their property and an equity stake in its capital value. This would in practice require central government to force recalcitrant (i.e. Labour-controlled) district councils to comply with the overall policy, and neither side would be eager for this to happen. The chances of obtaining uniformity across the country as a whole would therefore be remote.

37. John Fyfe and Andrew McCloud, 'Manpower Planning in Companies: General Lessons from a Number of Case Studies', *Department of Employment Gazette*, May 1978.

38. A survey by the Institute of Personnel Management in 1975, for example, concluded that 'manpower planning is not yet seen . . . as an area where both unions and employers can contribute together to the maximum utilization of human resources. Yet in the present-day climate with allegations of overmanning and the problems of growing redundancy, a greater degree of consultation and participation would seem to be essential.' – *Manpower Planning in Action*, IPM, 1975.

39. W. H. Beveridge, *Unemployment: A Problem of Industry*, Longmans, 1909, pp. 193–4.